I0166133

William M. (William Morris) Stewart

The evils of gold contraction

William M. (William Morris) Stewart

The evils of gold contraction

ISBN/EAN: 9783743314788

Manufactured in Europe, USA, Canada, Australia, Japa

Cover: Foto ©ninafisch / pixelio.de

Manufactured and distributed by brebook publishing software (www.brebook.com)

William M. (William Morris) Stewart

The evils of gold contraction

SPEECH

OF

HON. WM. M. STEWART,

OF NEVADA,

IN REPLY TO

THE HON. JOHN SHERMAN,

IN THE

SENATE OF THE UNITED STATES,

JUNE 1 AND 2, 1892.

———•◆•———

WASHINGTON.
1892.

·SPEECH

OF

HON. WILLIAM M. STEWART.

The Senate having under consideration the bill (S. 51) to provide for the free coinage of gold and silver bullion, and for other purposes—

Mr. STEWART said:

Mr. PRESIDENT: The Senator from Ohio [Mr. SHERMAN] has said that the silver question is an important question, and he has proved most conclusively that it is a far-reaching question, affecting the interests of all mankind. He has also shown that the present financial condition of the whole world is in a most critical and embarrassing state, so much so that he does not think the politicians ought to talk about it or ought to act upon it; that the whole question ought to be relegated to a few men of superior judgment and of superior wisdom; and of course he alluded to the gold monopoly. He deprecates discussion, after having made a speech of three hours and a half in length. Of course he is not on the list of politicians. He belongs to that sacred circle of financiers who have an intuition beyond their fellow-men. It is proper for him to discuss it and to make predictions.

In the course of my remarks I shall endeavor to show from the record that the Senator from Ohio is more responsible than any other living man for the disordered condition of the finances of the world, and that he has done more to injure the happiness and prosperity of the world than any other living man. If I do not succeed in accomplishing that before I sit down, I shall certainly convince myself of that fact, and I think I shall convince all those who listen to me.

He says, in the next place, that the condition of things, the agitation of this question, has produced distrust. How and why has it produced distrust? For the simple reason that the world is bankrupt upon a gold standard, and every man who is familiar with the finances of the world knows it, from the highest to the lowest, all the great ring of gold contractionists know it. It is admitted that there is not gold enough, and yet in the face of that admission it is proposed to make the balance of the world discard silver and use gold alone. The difficulty is that there are too many promises to pay and not enough gold with which to pay. The whole fabric is trembling everywhere, and that is what creates distrust.

It was said sneeringly that the reason why the lady in Mississippi, referred to by the Senator from Alabama [Mr. MORGAN] the other day, could not borrow $4,000 on 1,000 acres of good land which ordinarily would be worth from $50,000 to $100,000 was

3

the distrust which had arisen on account of this agitation. It was because the gold ring in New York know very well that it is impossible for that lady or any other farmer or producer, if he or she agrees to deliver gold, to obtain the gold to deliver. They know very well that they have gold in a corner, and that it can not be delivered. The reason why they will not lend money to anybody is because they know gold can not be procured for payment. They have it now in a corner, so that they know that the people can not get it, and that is the reason they will not loan it. If we would be quiet and allow them to continue contraction they intimate that the people might borrow money and pay gold, and pretend that it is the agitation which prevents them loaning money. They might make short loans with the idea that they could get them back before it was generally known that gold contraction means ruin.

The Senator tells us that the finances of this country have been more successful than in any other country in the history of man, and that this country is more prosperous than any other country that exists. Why should it not be so? Ours is the most productive country in the world. Its resources are unequaled. In enterprise its people have no competitors. Why should it not be more prosperous? But the Senator did not tell you that the iron grasp of contraction was equally heavy upon all the other nations of the world. He did not tell you that the people of Europe were in a worse condition than they have been for a half century. He did not tell you that starvation and misery exist throughout the Old World. Why should this condition exist? I will tell you why, and I wish the Senator from Ohio were not absent from his seat, for I shall speak of some things in regard to his own history that he may have forgotten.

He tells us further that the dollar was dropped from the mint act of 1873 on the petition of the Legislature of California. I have heard that remark from the Senator before. I have examined the entire journals of the Legislature of California. I have inquired for it in California, I have investigated that question, but I have never been able to find any such petition. I do not believe it is a fact. I undertook to interrupt the Senator from Ohio in order to have him refer me to that petition, but he declined to be interrupted. A petition for the discontinuance of the coinage of silver coming from California in 1873! It is impossible. Nothing of the kind occurred. The Senator can not produce it.

Before I am through I will show upon whose motion silver was demonetized, and I will again give the history of it in detail, so that the people may know who has brought upon them their present suffering, who has brought upon the country the present depression, who has disturbed the finances of the entire world, for it is all a matter of record.

The Senator from Ohio tells us that if he had known the consequences of the demonetization of silver he would have done the same that he did, but all the time he is attempting to drag others in and make them responsible. There are those who are not here to speak for themselves, but I shall refer to their testimony in order to place the responsibility for disturbing the finances of the world where it ought to be placed, and in order that it shall not rest upon the shoulders of those who did not participate in this great wrong.

He further tells us that the demonetization of silver was effected by the Democratic party in 1854, and that Jefferson had something to do with it; that the fathers, whose example we ought to follow, had something to do with it. To prove this he holds up before the Senate the coinage, and tells the Senate that there were only 8,000,000 silver dollars coined; that nobody was in favor of its coinage.

Now, I undertake to say there never was a year between 1793, when the Mint was opened, and 1873, the time of the passage of the mint act, when there was not legal-tender silver coined, and instead of there being only $8,000,000 there was over $140,000,000 of full legal-tender silver coined. It is true that some years they did not coin dollars, but in those years they coined half dollars and quarters, which up to 1852 were a full legal tender. We would be willing now to coin half dollars and to make them full legal tender.

I have the same book before me that he had, in which is contained the same list, and to show how disingenuous his statement was I commence here with 1793, and show that full legal-tender silver was coined every year from the opening of the Mint of the United States until the passage of the act of 1873; and in the aggregate, as I said, full legal-tender silver (for it makes no difference about the denomination, and the legal tender was unlimited and the weights were full) to the amount of $140,000,000 was coined.

Why did they not coin more? Because we were not producing silver. There was another reason, which was well set forth by the Senator from Missouri [Mr. COCKRELL] last year, and I shall take occasion in a moment to have a portion of his speech incorporated into mine. The reason was that until 1857 foreign coins, Spanish milled dollars, were on hand, and there were many other foreign coins on hand which were declared full legal tender in this country. In old colonial times there was a considerable amount of money in the country. It was not American coin that we had; it was Spanish milled dollars.

Mr. GEORGE. Which were made legal tender in this country.

Mr. STEWART. Yes; they were made legal tender in this country, and all of us know that when we were boys and had a coin nine times out of ten it was a foreign coin. The most of the coin that circulated among the people was foreign coin, but it was full legal tender. Then there was no necessity for coining so much, because the foreign coins came in here and were used. Coin was largely imported from Spanish America, and we declared it a legal tender, and there was a vast amount of it used. It was the money of the people.

But now we have declared that foreign coin shall not be a legal tender and have even excluded our own producers from the mints. That is the change which has taken place. During Mr. Jefferson's Administration and every other Administration full legal-tender silver was continuously coined and foreign silver was circulating here as a full legal tender. The people were never denied the right to use silver money as full legal tender or to have it coined as such until the act of 1873, when the great crime of the century was perpetrated.

I should like at this point to incorporate in my remarks an extract from the speech of the Senator from Missouri [Mr. COCKRELL], in which he gives an account of the foreign coin and the state of the law, and does it in better terms than I have the time to do now.

The PRESIDING OFFICER. The extract will be printed in the RECORD in the absence of objection.

The extract referred to is as follows:

Now, let us have the light of facts and figures and law upon this question, and see what was actually done from 1792 to the coinage act of February 12, 1873.

From 1792 to 1853, inclusive, we coined in our mints $75,961,554.90 of standard silver half-dollars, quarter-dollars, dimes, and half-dimes, consisting of 132,498,306 half-dollar pieces, 15,996,162 quarter-dollar pieces, 38,900,625 dimes, and 36,465,978 half-dimes, and aggregating 223,861,071 separate pieces, and being about nine separate pieces to each man, woman, and child of our population; and all these coins were, by law, a full legal tender in payment of all sums whatever equally with the standard silver dollar and gold coins.

Under the laws existing up to 1857 there was no necessity, no use, no reason for the coinage of such dollars. By the common law, the resolves of the Continental Congress and of the Congress of the Confederation already quoted, gold and silver coins were current and legal tenders at about the ratio of 1 to 15, and no United States coins were minted prior to 1792. Among the first laws passed by Congress under the Constitution was that of July 31, 1789, to regulate the collection of duties, which prescribed the rates at which foreign coins and currency should be estimated as money, and made them receivable for all duties and debts at such rates, and from that date almost continuously up to February 21, 1857, foreign coins of gold and silver, and particularly the Spanish milled dollar and the Mexican dollar, were made current and receivable for all public dues and a legal tender for all demands at the rates declared in such laws, the Spanish milled dollar and the Mexican dollar being estimated at 100 cents, or $1.

These foreign-coined silver dollars answered every purpose of our own silver dollars, and, consequently very few silver dollars were coined prior to 1857. During the war, beginning in 1861 and up to 1879, our money was a paper currency. In 1868 the silver bullion in the standard dollar was worth 2.57 cents more than the gold dollar, and we coined 54,800 silver dollars. In 1869 the silver dollar was worth 2.47 cents more than the gold dollar, and we coined 231,350 silver dollars. In 1870 the silver dollar was worth 2.67 cents more than the gold dollar, and we coined 588,308 silver dollars. In 1871 the silver dollar was worth 2.57 cents more than the gold dollar, and we coined 657,929 silver dollars.

In 1872 the silver dollar was worth 2.25 cents more than the gold dollar, and yet we coined 1,112,961 silver dollars, being the largest number of silver dollars ever coined in any year since the establishment of the Mint. In the year 1873, up to the passage of the coinage act of February 12, stopping the further coinage of the standard silver dollar, that dollar was worth forty-six-one-hundredths of 1 cent more than the gold dollar, and we coined in the one month and twelve days of that year 977,150 silver dollars.

During these five years one month and twelve days from 1868 to February 12, 1873, we coined 3,622,496 standard silver dollars, being 45 per cent of our total coinage of such dollars up to said last date.

These figures show conclusively the increasing coinage of the standard dollar up to the day its coinage was stopped by law, beginning soon after the close of the war and after the law prohibiting the further currency and legal tender of foreign silver coins in this country.

Mr. STEWART. So much for the Democratic party or the Republican party or any other party demonetizing silver previous to 1873. Before I go to the history of that, I do not want to overlook any position taken by the Senator from Ohio, and consequently in following him my speech will be desultory and disarranged.

The Senator says that if the present law leads to disaster and silver continues to fall in price we would get too much silver and silver coinage would have to be stopped. That is the old story. I think that he will have to consult the American people before he stops it, and when he stops it I think he will have to do something else that will be satisfactory to the people of the country.

He tells us that the movements in Europe tend towards the utter disuse of silver; that all the European nations are being brought into it and adopting the gold standard because it is better, and still he advises a conference. If there is such a movement going on, let them proceed with it.

The Senator says all our legislation has been tentative and experimental. Certainly it has been experimental. The money-getting and the money-manipulating class wanted a law to speculate under, and the Senator gave it to them. What we object to is tentative legislation. We want to return to the money of the fathers. That was not tentative. We want to return to the money which has existed from prehistoric ages.

Was the act of 1873 tentative? If it was, we have had enough of it. We say that we are sick of tentative measures, measures under which men can speculate, measures by which the wealth of the country has been transferred from the masses who produce it to the few who absorb it. Nothing can be a greater condemnation of the policy than that we have been trying experiments that were temporary and tentative. In every experiment the people have lost and the money-changers have gained.

Look at the flow of wealth from the many to the few under this tentative system. The Senator says the agitation, the protest against this tentative system is a threat that the people do not submit, and that it is dangerous. He talks about selling our silver. Some Senator asked him under what law, and he did not wish to answer and declined to be interrupted.

The silver which has been purchased under the act of 1890 will remain in the Treasury until it is coined, although the present Secretary will not coin it as provided in the law for the purpose of redeeming the Treasury notes, but threatens to sell bonds and buy gold for that purpose. No Administration and no party will ever be tolerated in increasing the national debt for the purpose of buying gold and allow the silver which has been purchased for the purpose of redemption to lie idle in the Treasury. That would be folly. The Secretary of the Treasury has no law to do it, and there is no public sentiment in its favor. It can not be done.

The Senator asks is it possible for the United States to raise the silver of the world, amounting to nearly four thousand millions, from its market price to par, and declares that the United States would be compelled to take it all. Is that true? Is there any mass of silver of that description which can come here and which we would be compelled to take? First, he tells us that free coinage will reduce the price of the dollar to the present market price of bullion. The present market price is more than 30 per cent discount. All the silver in the world is circulating as a full legal tender where it exists at a higher valuation than our silver, except in Mexico, which has a ratio of 16½ to 1, and in Japan which has a ratio a little in excess of ours, 16.518. Except the coins of these two countries, all the silver coin in the world is rated higher than ours.

The Senator says we should have to take all that silver, and that our silver dollar would remain depreciated. Would foreigners bring their silver here if our silver did not go up? Why do they not take it to India; why not take it to Mexico? There is free coinage in India. France is dealing with India, and the average balance of trade is thirty-three millions per annum against France and in favor of India, and has been for the last twenty years. She did not send her silver there. Does she want to get rid of it? If so, why does she not send it there and have it coined into rupees? The rupee is just as valuable as our dollar according to the argument of the Senator from Ohio. He says our dollar will be at 30 per cent discount, and rupees are at 30 per cent discount now as compared with gold.

Would there be any inducement to send it here? There are eleven hundred millions of full legal-tender silver coin circulating in Europe at a ratio of 15½ to 1, which is more than 3 per cent higher than the silver in our silver coin is valued. They would lose 3 per cent if they brought it here for coinage. If silver coin remains at the bullion price, as asserted by the Senator, they would lose 33½ per cent by bringing it to the United States for coinage. At that rate they would lose one-third of the eleven hundred millions they have if they were compelled to bring their coined silver here. What object or what inducement would there be to bring it to this country? If it be true, as asserted by the Senator from Ohio, that free coinage would not advance the price of silver, what object could be gained by bringing it here?

The Senator read from an argument of the Director of the Mint in the North American Review to the effect that ships would be loaded with silver to be brought here. Whoever heard of such nonsense as that? Unless our silver dollar goes higher than their silver nobody will bring silver here. Coined silver in Europe is worth $1.33 an ounce, and under free coinage ours will be worth only $1.2929 if we maintain it at par. The Senator says that silver coin will fall in value to the present market price of silver bullion. Why will they send it here if such be the case? They would lose over 30 per cent by doing so. France has had a test of that question very recently, and it ought to be a lesson to us.

In 1885 the Latin Union met and agreed to dissolve in five years, and when they dissolved each country agreed to redeem in gold coin its silver held by the others, but to accomplish that it was required that there should be a year's notice. The time ran out in November, 1890. None of the nations of that Union gave the required notice. There was a great clamor to make France give notice. What was the reason assigned why France would not give notice and take $1.33 an ounce for her silver? I might state that at that time France had 600,000,000 francs or $120,000,000, of the silver coin of the other countries, which she might have exchanged for gold at $1.33 an ounce.

What is the reason assigned for not doing it? The financiers of France said that in France there were nearly $700,000,000 of legal-tender silver among the people, and if she should sell her silver for gold she would destroy the confidence of the people in their money and produce distress and contraction. That she would not do, and she holds it still. She was unwilling to produce the disasters which would follow such a performance.

It is perfectly obvious that if France would not sell her silver to Italy, Belgium, Greece, and Switzerland for $1.33 an ounce she would not be likely to send it here to have it coined into our money at a loss of 33 per cent, which would be the case if silver remained at its present market price. as asserted by the Senator from Ohio. This is the foundation of the arguments of the gold contractionists.

• Then the Senator said that all securities in this country are based on gold. I deny it. I admit that he and his co-workers have labored in season and out of season to secure that end, but every obligation of the United States is payable in either gold or silver coin at the option of the Government. Although no Administration has obeyed the law in that respect, it is nevertheless true, and the assertion that the Government securities are payable in gold is false and has no foundation in fact. There is no statute of that kind.

Then the Senator from Ohio speaks of the making of gold contracts.

Mr. GEORGE. Has the Government any such contracts?

Mr. STEWART. The Government has no contracts agreeing to pay in gold. All contracts are payable in either gold or silver at the option of the Government; but our Government will not exercise the option. The Government gives that to the creditor. The creditor is the only favored class in our Government; the money-loaner is the only person to be considered, and to him the option is given. In France the Government exercises the option, and pays her obligations in either gold or silver, which is most convenient for the Government. In this country the Administration has refused the Government the option, given it to the creditor, and disparaged silver in every possible way.

The Senator from Ohio speaks of gold contracts, and he alludes to the fact that some mortgages were taken in my name as mortgagee, payable in gold. That was explained several times. A very unfortunate law was passed during the war in California and Nevada, allowing specific contracts payable in gold. The law was aimed against the greenback. It was unfortunate for California, because it shut out immigration to that country for fifteen years. No man would stand the discount; people would not visit that section, and it was isolated and shut off from the balance of the world for fifteen years. There was no immigration, no visiting that country, and it was utterly paralyzed. It was not until the moneys of the country were made equal that people would go there. Then immigration went.

The gold-contract law was a very prejudicial law, and worked hard against the people. Merchants bought goods with greenbacks and sold them for gold, making thereby colossal fortunes. I protested against that law from the first. I happened, however, to order the sale of some property in Alameda by a firm of brokers who were engaged in business there, and they had the contracts made on their printed forms, which they have kept to this day. I never asked to have a gold contract made. I never used one made to my knowledge, and would not demand any such thing; but it was in accordance with the ordinary commercial business of the country to have contracts made in that way.

The Senator from Ohio is continually referring to Mexico. I undertake to say that Mexico is in a more prosperous condition comparatively than we are. If she had not free coinage she would have been bankrupt long ago. Everybody said she would be bankrupt when she incurred such vast obligations for railroad subsidies, but free coinage has given her money with which to do something, and the silver dollar has the same purchasing power there that it had before silver was demonetized. Mexico is now attracting manufacturers from this country. Five large smelting reduction works were built there in the last year because Mexico had free coinage and because the works could be carried on more prosperously than they could here.

When I was in Mexico last summer there were several men interested in manufacturing who were looking to the establishment of manufactories because they can do business there better, for the reason that money was more plentiful. Mexico is not suffering on account of free coinage; it is free coinage which is saving that country. No people can prosper without money. We are fighting against the fates. We are doing a little better than they are in Europe, but we are doing worse than we ought to.

The Senator tells us that there was a large amount of silver coinage under the resumption act. I deny that there was legal tender silver coined under the resumption act. We retired the fractional currency and substituted token silver money of a limited legal-tender quality and used it the same as we did the nickel; but we dishonored it. We did not coin any legal-tender money under that act.

Then the Senator speaks of protection. Is protection wedded to gold monopoly? Is protection wedded to contraction? Is protection wedded to the prostration of the industries of the country? I have voted for protection; my section has stood by the Republican party and protection, but we never heard that protection to American labor and protection to gold sharks meant the same thing; and when the people of the West are informed that protection and gold contraction belong together it will be hard for those starving people to be brought up to the line of protection. A severer blow could not have been struck by the Senator from Ohio at the protection system than to have proclaimed that it was part of the gold-standard theory.

The Senator would change the ratio, and yesterday he said it ought to be about 23 or 24 to 1. To-day he settled down to the ratio of 23 to 1. The people are told they can have their constitutional rights, they can have the money of the Constitution, provided they will give the gold trust 33⅓ per cent for it, and on no other terms. That is the proposition. Besides, the Senator proposes to increase its weight 33⅓ per cent and destroy the use of silver as money.

Mr. MITCHELL. May I ask the Senator a question?

Mr. STEWART. Yes.

Mr. MITCHELL. Would not one of the effects of the increase of the ratio to twenty-three and a fraction be an increase in the value of bonds, of farm mortgages, notes, and other evidences of debt in the hands of the creditors of the country to an amount equal to the difference between the value of the silver now in the silver dollar and the amount proposed to be put in?

Mr. STEWART. That is just why it is being done; that is what makes these men take to it; that is the very object of it. You never see any proposition made by the gold trust that has not something of that kind in it. No fair proposition is made by them, nothing that can stand the light of day is suggested by them; but it is always something which will enable them further to oppress the people. It must have an element of robbery in it to give it zest and make it philosophical.

Mr. McPHERSON. Will the Senator yield to me a moment?

Mr. STEWART. I should rather not yield, because these interruptions make my speech too long, and there are many things that I intend to say.

Mr. McPHERSON. The Senator is very earnest in this matter, but I want to call his attention to the converse of the proposition suggested by the Senator from Oregon [Mr. MITCHELL]. I will not, however, interfere.

Mr. STEWART. I should prefer not to be interrupted now, because I have still a great deal of matter here. I know my remarks are very scattering, but the fallacies which have been uttered ought to be exploded.

Before I leave the point on which I have been dwelling, I wish to call attention to the fact that nothing has occurred since the crime of 1873, to suggest a change of ratio by putting more silver in the silver coin in proportion to gold. On the contrary, the silver production of the world has made a very different suggestion. I quote from Chevalier, who was a celebrated French writer:

From the date of the discovery of America until 1848, Chevalier estimates the production of gold and silver respectively as follows:

	Silver.	Gold.
From America	$5,261,000,000	$1,998,000,000
From elsewhere	444,000,000	628,000,000
Total	5,705,000,000	2,626,000,000

The gold supply was 31 per cent of the whole.
The production from the beginning in America was, according to Humboldt:

	Silver.	Gold.
From America	£7,071,831	£2,382,315
From elsewhere	661,145	251,822
Total	7,732,976	2,634,137

This is on the French basis of valuing the metals at 15½ to 1. The gold supply was only 31 per cent, and the silver supply was 69 per cent during all that period, and still the ratio never got above 15½ to 1. It was maintained through all the ages in that way. Why was it? Because very few people used gold. The great mass of the people of the world use silver, and thus the ratio was kept in that way. That was the coinage ratio, and it remained permanent from 1801, according to another statistician, until 1873.

I have in my hand a table showing the relative price of gold and silver on the ratio of 15½ to 1 from 1800 to 1873. In France the two metals remained the same; the parity was kept up. It was maintained permanently, because as long as France would give the same amount of money for 15½ ounces of silver that she would give for an ounce of gold, and her mints were open to receive it, the parity was sustained for seventy-three years.

The table is taken from the Financial and Mining Record of New York, and is as follows:

XXIV.—THE FIXITY OF THE RATIO OF 15.5 TO 1 DEMONSTRATED BY FACTS.

For the demonstration of a truth, facts are worth more than authorities, howsoever imposing these may happen to be. The prices of silver noted at London by the Messrs. Abel and Pixley and reproduced by Soetbeer, demonstrate that the unrestricted coinage of gold and silver in France at the ratio of 1 to 15½ clearly sufficed to maintain the price of silver in London and, therefore, upon the commercial markets of the world at about 60⅞ pence per ounce troy standard metal—that is to say, at a price corresponding to the French ratio of 1 to 15½ between 1803-1873. The departures from above or below that price explain themselves, as we shall show, by the cost of sending silver whether from London to Paris or, in turn, from Paris to London. We give below the variation in prices of silver as reported by Soetbeer:

	Mean price.	Highest.	Lowest.		Mean price.	Highest.	Lowest.
1800	60 1/8	......	......	1837	59 9/16	60 3/8	59
1801	61	......	......	1838	59 1/2	60 1/8	59 3/4
1802	61 13/16	......	......	1839	60 3/8	60 5/8	60
1803	61 3/16	......	......	1840	60 3/8	60 3/4	60 1/8
1804	61 3/16	......	......	1841	60 1/16	60 3/8	59 3/4
1805	59 3/4	......	......	1842	59 7/16	59 3/4	59 1/8
1806	60 3/4	......	......	1843	59 3/16	59 3/4	59
1807	61 1/8	......	......	1844	59 1/2	59 3/4	59 1/4
1808	58 7/8	......	......	1845	59 1/4	59 7/8	58 7/8
1809	59 1/16	......	......	1846	59 5/16	60 1/8	59
1810	59 13/16	......	......	1847	59 11/16	60 5/8	58 7/8
1811	60 11/16	......	......	1848	59 1/2	60	58 1/2
1812	58 1/2	......	......	1849	59 3/4	60 1/4	59 1/2
1813	58	......	......	1850	60 1/16	61 1/2	59 1/2
1814	62 11/16	......	......	1851	61	61 5/8	90
1815	61 13/16	......	......	1852	60 1/2	61 7/8	50 7/8
1816	61 11/16	......	......	1853	61 1/2	62 3/8	60 5/8
1817	61 9/16	......	......	1854	61 1/2	61 7/8	60 7/8
1818	61 7/16	......	......	1855	61 5/16	61 5/8	60
1819	61 1/2	......	......	1856	61 5/16	62 1/4	60 1/2
1820	60 5/8	62 1/2	59 1/2	1857	61 3/4	62 3/8	61
1821	59 5/8	59 1/2	58 1/2	1858	61 5/16	61 7/8	60 3/4
1822	59 11/16	60	59	1859	62 1/16	62 3/4	61 3/4
1823	59 1/4	59 1/4	58 3/4	1860	61 11/16	62 3/8	61 1/4
1824	59 5/8	60 1/2	59 1/2	1861	60 3/16	61 3/8	60 1/8
1825	60 1/16	61 1/4	60 1/2	1862	61 7/16	62 1/8	61
1826	59 13/16	61	58 3/4	1863	61 3/8	61 3/4	61
1827	59 13/16	60 1/4	59 1/4	1864	51 3/8	62 1/2	60 7/8
1828	59 3/4	60 1/2	59 1/4	1865	61 1/16	61 7/8	60 1/8
1829	59 3/4	60	59 1/2	1866	61 1/8	62 1/4	60 3/8
1830	59 5/8	60	59 1/4	1867	60 9/16	61 1/4	60 5/16
1831	60	60 7/8	60	1868	62 1/2	61 1/8	60 1/8
1832	59 13/16	60 1/4	59 3/4	1869	60 7/16	61	60 1/4
1833	59 7/16	60	59 3/4	1870	60 9/16	62	60
1834	59 13/16	60 3/8	59 3/4	1871	60 1/2	60 7/8	60 3/16
1835	59 11/16	60	59 1/2	1872	60 5/16	61 1/8	59 1/4
1836	60	60 3/8	59 3/8				

In 1873 there came the demonetization of silver in Germany, with an accumulation of silver in France at the mint for from twelve to fourteen months, from which occurred a loss of interest of from 4 to 5 per cent, and a suspension, in fact, of unrestricted coinage, even before legislative restrictions were imposed.

Our figures show that except during the years 1812 and 1813, when commercial relations between bimetallic France and England were almost completely interrupted, the variations in the price of silver were maintained within the limits of the cost of transportation of the metal, whether from London to Paris or from Paris to London.

From 1803 even up to 1850 remittances from London to Paris were made chiefly in silver, the selling or market price of which at London was such as would bear the cost of transportation to Paris; on the other hand, however, from 1850 up to 1870 remittances were chiefly made in gold, while silver was drawn from Paris to London, and when in turn the price of silver in London appreciated sufficiently to cover the cost of its transmission thither from Paris, but all the same the bimetallic par remained unaffected.

This fact is all the more remarkable because of the unprecedented occurrences meanwhile in connection with the relative production of the precious metals, and in despite of which the relative money value almost invariably remained materially the same. This fact of itself affords the most striking evidence that really the relative value of the two metals has in no wise depended on their relative volume of production.

From 1801 to 1840 the production of gold was $444,502,000 and of silver $1,121,370,000, making gold 28.387 per cent and silver 71.613; so that the proportion from 1801 to 1840 was very nearly the same as the average production during the whole period from the discovery of America until 1848. From 1840 to 1850 the production was more nearly equal. The percentage was a little more of gold than silver on account of gold discoveries in Russia, and it was 52 to 47 and a fraction.

In this connection the translator may here usefully or instructively append the following table of the relative production of gold and silver during this century, the data being mainly derived from Soetbeer:

	Amount.	Per cent.
1801 to 1840.		
Gold	$414,502,000	28.387
Silver	1,121,370,000	71.613
Total	1,565,872,000	100.000
1841 to 1850.		
Gold	363,917,304	52.866
Silver	324,457,536	47.134
Total	688,374,840	100.000

I here append a table showing the ratio of production of gold and silver from 1851 to 1890, both inclusive:

Statement of the annual production of gold and silver in the world from 1851 to 1890, inclusive.

Year.	Gold.	Silver.	Aggregate.	Average per year for five years.
1851	$67,600,000	$40,000,000	$107,600,000	
1852	132,750,000	40,600,000	173,350,000	
1853	155,450,000	40,600,000	196,050,000	$164,145,000
1854	127,450,000	40,600,000	168,050,000	
1855	135,075,000	40,600,000	175,675,000	

Statement of the annual production of gold and silver—Continued.

Year.	Gold.	Silver.	Aggregate.	Average per year for five years.
1856	$147,600,000	$40,650,000	$188,250,000	
1857	133,275,000	40,650,000	173,925,000	
1858	124,650,000	40,650,000	165,300,000	$170,625,000
1859	124,850,000	40,750,000	155,600,000	
1860	119,250,000	40,800,000	160,050,000	
1861	113,800,000	44,700,000	158,500,000	
1862	107,750,000	45,200,000	152,950,000	
1863	106,950,000	49,200,000	156,150,000	160,890,000
1864	113,000,000	51,700,000	164,700,000	
1865	120,200,000	51,950,000	172,150,000	
1866	121,100,000	50,750,000	171,850,000	
1867	104,025,000	54,225,000	158,250,000	
1868	109,725,000	50,225,000	159,950,000	160,440,000
1869	106,225,000	47,500,000	153,725,000	
1870	106,850,000	51,575,000	158,425,000	
1871	107,000,000	61,050,000	168,050,000	
1872	99,600,000	62,250,000	161,850,000	
1873	96,200,000	81,800,000	178,000,000	169,630,000
1874	90,750,000	71,500,000	162,250,000	
1875	97,500,000	80,500,000	178,000,000	
1876	103,700,000	87,600,000	191,300,000	
1877	114,000,000	81,000,000	195,000,000	
1878	119,000,000	95,000,000	214,000,000	201,700,000
1879	109,000,000	96,000,000	205,000,000	
1880	106,500,000	96,700,000	203,200,000	
1881	103,000,000	102,000,000	205,000,000	
1882	102,000,000	111,800,000	213,800,000	
1883	95,400,000	115,300,000	210,700,000	212,720,120
1884	101,700,600	105,500,000	207,200,600	
1885	108,400,000	118,500,000	226,900,000	
1886	106,000,000	120,600,000	226,600,000	
1887	107,000,000	125,500,000	232,500,000	
1888	106,000,000	142,400,000	246,400,000	254,060,500
1889	122,438,500	159,678,000	282,116,500	
1890	116,009,000	166,677,000	282,686,000	
Total	4,388,772,500	2,963,280,000	7,473,053,100	

The relative proportion from 1851 to 1890 was 60 per cent of gold to 40 per cent of silver on the ratio of 16 to 1, as shown by the reports of the Director of the Mint. From the discovery of this country until 1848 the production of the two metals was, gold 31, silver 69. Still it is said that the overproduction of silver is the reason why the price has gone down. Never in the history of the world has the production of silver been so small in comparison with that of gold as it has been for the last forty years. If the ratio were to be changed on production it would be reduced to about 10 to 1 or 11 to 1, as I said the other day.

Then what has deprived silver of its value? It is not an increased production as compared with gold. All the facts are the other way. I shall show what has disparaged silver and who did it before I get through.

Mr. President, there has been nothing in nature to effect this terrible condition of the finances of the world. On the contrary, no generation of men was ever so blessed as the people who have lived in the last forty years, so far as the bounties of nature are concerned. Empires and civilizations have appeared and disappeared with production and failure of mines. The history of every nation which has risen can be written by the history of the mines of gold and silver from which it obtained its supply. We can trace now by modern investigation where Egypt got her gold when she built the Pyramids.

The ruins of Nubia furnish ample proof. We know that the various nations of Western Asia have prospered by their mines; we see where they got their money, and one after another disappeared as the money failed. We know where Rome, when her conquering legions subdued the world, got the money she had. According to Gibbon and others, nearly two thousand millions of gold and silver coin were in circulation in the Roman Empire in the time of Augustus, besides a vast amount of plate and ornaments. That money was lost, dissipated, worn out, buried, and hidden in her commotions until her people became abject slaves. They established the feudal system by farm mortgages, as they are now doing in this country. The farms were gradually delivered up to the mortgagees, and the mortgagees became the feudal lords. There was no attempt to revive civilization until gold and silver came from the New World. It was the gold and silver from America that inspired the manhood of the people of Europe, which had been lost by poverty.

A man without money is a coward. Our farmers are becoming cowards; our business men are becoming cowards; they are becoming the slaves of the creditor. Few men are brave enough to walk along the street owing a tailor's bill which they can not pay. There is no lady who visits the shops who does not feel embarrassed in a dry-goods store if there is no money in her purse. The want of money engenders cowardice, but money inspires its possessor with the power of resistance. You may kick a tramp from your door, but put $200 dollars in his pocket and you will treat him very differently. I have seen this often in the mining country. I have seen a poor unfortunate driven from his boarding-house, kicked out of saloons, and who would cringe to everybody, but let him strike a bonanza and come into town, and he would sacrifice his life for his honor. The transformation would be miraculous. The Reformation did not begin until the people got some money to go to the conferences. The object was to keep the people away. They were poor and could not attend, and none but money kings could be there.

The system by which the future is mortgaged to secure promises to pay money and then by subtle contrivances the value of money is enhanced, is the most dangerous to liberty of any system invented by man. We passed through a terrible ordeal in consequence of slavery; we made sacrifices which no other people in the world ever made, but in abolishing slavery and liberating four millions of slaves we commenced forging the chains to bind all the white people in the world in bonds more galling, in slavery more degrading, than African slavery. African slavery did not compare with the abject condition of the people in a state of feudalism.

515

See what is being done in this country. The value of money is increasing every day. The indebtedness of the country at any one time is estimated at not less than $30,000,000,000. I mean the whole indebtedness of the people. You double that, you take away the means of payment at the same time, and the far-reaching and terrible effects can not be comprehended.

A gold dollar is worth to-day as much as two gold dollars were before the crime of 1873 was perpetrated. We are laboring against a power which we can not resist. If it can not be resisted in this Chamber, if the representatives of the people bow to it, it can not be resisted in any part of the world.

Why send ambassadors to Europe to consult as to how tight the chains shall be drawn upon the people? Has it come to this that, we can not have a money system of our own? Political independence without financial independence is a sham. Are we to go to Europe to ask their permission to have a financial policy of our own? Our evils come from Europe; the chains were forged on the other side of the Atlantic, as I will show you.

Now, let us look a little at the history of the demonetization of silver, and see whether the people of California were responsible for it. In 1867 there was a monetary conference held at Paris to consider the unification of the currency. Nobody in this country realized what it was or what was going to be done, or that there was anything wicked about it. After considerable discussion, the conference recommended the demonetization of silver and the adoption of the gold standard, although the proposition met with much opposition, because silver was at that time more valuable than gold. I have the report of the commission here. You will find it in Senate Executive Document 1624, second session of the Fortieth Congress, and it runs through many pages. I want to call attention to one particular letter.

The then chairman of the Committee on Finance of the United States Senate visited London. He certainly visited Paris, because here is a letter dated at a hotel in that city. It is addressed to Mr. Ruggles, and is signed JOHN SHERMAN. It is dated at Hotel Jardin des Tuileries, May 18, 1867. This letter advocated the adoption of a single gold standard most enthusiastically. I will ask to have this letter, which is a Simon pure gold-standard letter of the first description, printed in my remarks, so that everybody can read it. I shall not take time to read it now; but it was written for the purpose of advocating and did advocate the adoption of the single gold standard:

HOTEL JARDIN DES TUILLERIES, *May 18, 1867.*

MY DEAR SIR: Your note of yesterday, inquiring whether Congress would probably, in future coinage, make our gold dollar conform in value to the gold 5-franc piece, has been received.

There has been so little discussion in Congress upon the subject that I can not base my opinion upon anything said or done there.

The subject has, however, excited the attention of several important commercial bodies in the United States, and the time is now so favorable that I feel quite sure that Congress will adopt any practical measure that will secure to the commercial world a uniform standard of value and exchange.

The only question will be how this can be accomplished.

The treaty of December 23, 1865, between France, Italy, Belgium, and Switzerland, and the probable acquiescence in that treaty of Prussia, has laid the foundation for such a standard. If Great Britain will reduce the value of her sovereign 2 pence, and the United States will reduce the value of her dollar something over 3 cents. we then have a coinage in the franc. dollar, and sovereign, easily computed, and which will readily pass in all countries; the dollar as 5 francs, and the sovereign as 25 francs.

This will put an end to the loss and intricacies of exchange and discount. Our gold dollar is certainly as good a unit of value as the franc; and so the English think of their pound sterling. These coins are now exchangeable only at a considerable loss, and this exchange is a profit only to brokers and bankers. Surely each commercial nation should be willing to yield a little to secure a gold coin of equal value, weight, and diameter, from whatever mint it may have been issued.

As the gold 5-franc piece is now in use by over sixty millions of people of several different nationalities, and is of convenient form and size, it may well be adopted by other nations as the common standard of value; leaving to each nation to regulate the divisions of this unit in silver coins or tokens.

If this be done, France will surely abandon the impossible effort of making two standards of value. Gold coins will answer all the purposes of European commerce. A common gold standard will regulate silver coinage, of which the United States will furnish the greater part, especially for the Chinese trade.

In England many persons of influence and different chambers of commerce are earnestly in favor of the proposed change in their coinage. The change is so slight with them that an enlightened self-interest will soon induce them to make it, especially if we make the greater change in our coinage. We will have some difficulty in adjusting existing contracts with the new dollar; but as contracts are now based upon the fluctuating value of paper money, even the reduced dollar in coin will be of more purchasable value than our currency.

We can easily adjust the reduction with the public creditors in the payment or conversion of their securities, while private creditors might be authorized to recover upon the old standard. All these are matters of detail to which I hope the commission will direct their attention.

I have thought a good deal of how the object you propose may be most readily accomplished. It is clear that the United States can not become a party to the treaty referred to. They could not agree upon the silver standard; nor could we limit the amount of our coinage, as proposed by the treaty. The United States is so large in extent, is so sparsely populated, and the price of labor is so much higher than in Europe, that we require more currency per capita. We now produce the larger part of the gold and silver of the world, and can not limit our coinage, except by the wants of our people and the demands of commerce.

Congress alone can change the value of our coin. I see no object in negotiating with other powers on the subject. As coin is now in general circulation with us, we can readily fix by law the size, weight, and measure of future issues. It is not worth while to negotiate about that which we can do without negotiation, and we do not wish to limit ourselves to treaty restrictions.

And now, my dear sir, allow me to say in conclusion, that I heartily sympathize with you and others in your efforts to secure the adoption of the metrical system of weights and measures.

The tendency of the age is to break down all needless restrictions upon social and commercial intercourse. Nations are now as much akin to each other as provinces were of old. Prejudices disappear by contact. People of different nations learn to respect each other as they find that their differences are the effect of social and local customs not founded upon good reasons. I trust that the Industrial Commission will enable the world to compute the value of all productions by the same standard, to measure by the same yard or meter, and weigh by the same scales.

Such a result would be of greater value than the usual employments of diplomatists and statesmen.

I am very truly yours,   JOHN SHERMAN.

(Senate Executive Document No. 14, Fortieth Congress, second session.)

The monetary conference then in session at Paris recommended the single gold standard. This recommendation was secured through the efforts of Mr. Ruggles, backed up by the letter of the chairman of the Finance Committee of the American Senate.

Mr. GEORGE. Who was Ruggles?

Mr. STEWART. The American commissioner to the conference, which was held in Paris to unify weights and measures.

515—2

That was in August. Then in the January following—January, 1868—the following took place in the Senate:

Mr. SHERMAN asked, and by unanimous consent obtained, leave to bring in the following bill; which was read twice, referred to the Committee on Finance, and ordered to be printed.

I will not read the whole bill, but I will read the third section, which contains the gist of the whole matter:

SEC. 3. *And be it further enacted*, That the gold coins to be issued under this act shall be a legal tender in all payments to any amount; and the silver coins shall be a legal tender to an amount not exceeding $10 in any one payment.

Mr. GEORGE. What was the date?

Mr. STEWART. It was introduced in the Senate January 6, 1868. The bill was referred to the Committee on Finance. I wish to show the action of that committee. It was reported to the Senate June 9, 1868, and the report will be found in Senate Ex. Doc. No. 1629, second session of the Fortieth Congress, commencing on page 1 of the document. The report elaborately sets forth the reasons of the single gold standard, claimed great credit for it, eulogized the idea, and in fact goes so far as to exhibit a little jealousy that any foreigner should have any credit for it. It says:

The single standard of gold is an American idea, yielded reluctantly by France and other countries, where silver is the chief standard of value.

The debate in that monetary conference will show that that is a truthful statement and the idea was strongly combated by Europe. They hesitated very much but they yielded to Mr. SHERMAN'S American argument for the single gold standard. Mr. SHERMAN'S bill was a plain proposition to demonetize silver, but it met defeat. Mr. E. D. Morgan was a member of the committee. He was a Senator from New York, a man with a clear head, an honest, square man. He wrote a minority report, which killed the bill, and it was never called up for action. Among other things, on page 8, he said:

A change in our national coinage so grave as that proposed by the bill should be made only after the most mature deliberation. The circulating medium is a matter that directly concerns the affairs of every-day life, affecting not only the varied, intricate, and multiform interests of the people at home, to the minutest detail, but the relations of the nation with all other countries as well. The United States has a peculiar interest in such a question. It is a principal producer of the precious metals, and its geographical position, most favorable in view of impending commercial changes, renders it wise that we should be in no haste to fetter ourselves by any new international regulation based on an order of things belonging essentially to the past.

In another place he says:

The movement proposed in the bill appears to be in the wrong direction. The standard value of gold coin should be increased.

The standard value of gold, he says—

should be brought up to our own rather than lowered. The reason must be obvious. Authorities unite in the conclusion that a fall in the value of the precious metals, in consequence of their rapidly increasing quantity, is inevitable.

He says again, speaking of silver:

It is a favorite metal, entering into all transactions of daily life, and deserves proper recognition in any monetary system.

This is a most able report, which absolutely shows that tentative legislation was not the kind of legislation which ought to

be enacted, and then the bill was dropped. How to get the meas-
sure through then became a serious matter. It required cunning. A fair proposition of that kind had been kill d by the
ruthless logic and common sense of E. D. Morgan. John J. Knox,
who has been quoted as authority here, was the Comptroller of
the Currency at that time, and a plan was conceived to codify
the mint laws in which those experts knew very well that the
list of coins would not be particularly observed. This was in 1868.
Early in 1869 the first mint bill was introduced by Mr. SHER-
MAN, which omitted the silver dollar. It was an elaborate bill,
too cumbersome almost to read, one of those long codifying bills.
It was reported to the Senate and came up for discussion in January, 1870. The discussion was directed to the salaries of the
officers, because it created a mint bureau. Many of us partici-
pated in the discussion. Finally the Senator from Ohio [Mr.
SHERMAN], the chairman of the committee, proposed to charge
a se gniorage, to place a mint charge upongold and silver to be
coined. That was resisted by a good many of us on the obvious
ground that if the mints of Europe were opened to free coinage
it would be an inducement to export our bullion and not to coin it;
that it would be worth more in another country. On a yea-and-
nay vote the Senator from Ohio was beaten. He then practically abandoned the bill, and the yeas and nays were called,
and it was passed. The fact that there was an omission in the
list of coins was not observed or alluded to.

Mr. ALDRICH. Will it interrupt the Senator if I ask him a
question?

The PRESIDING OFFICER. Does the Senator from Nevada
yield to the Senator from Rhode Island?

Mr. STEWART. I will yield for a question. I do not want
to be interrupted much. I want to put this statement in together.

Mr. ALDRICH. I should like to ask the Senator what was
the attitude of the representatives from the Pacific coast on the
question of a gold standard at that time?

Mr. STEWART. Our attitude was against the single gold
standard. It was never called to our attention. Nobody dared
advocate it publicly. This bill was brought in evidently, I
should say, for the purpose of concealing the whole matter.
What we voted for was for the free coinage of both metals.
But then there came some other proceedings. I will not review
the proceedings in the other House, because there was a scattering discussion and nobody knew what the bill was. I have gone
through with that, but it is too lengthy for repetition.

The act of 1873 came from the other House. It was referred
to the Committee on Finance of the Senate. It was reported
back with certain amendments, a large number of amendments.
It was called up and partially read on the 16th of January. Mr.
SHERMAN remarked in calling it up:

I move that the Senate now proceed to the consideration of the mint bill,
as it is commonly called, revising and amending the laws relative to the
mints and assay offices and coinage of the United States. I do not think it
will take more than the time consumed in the reading of it.

The motion was agreed to; and the Senate, as in Committee of the Whole,
proceeded to consider the bill (H. R. 2934) revising and amending the laws
relative to the mints and assay offices and coinage of the United States.

The Secretary proceeded to read the bill, but before concluding the morning hour expired. When the bill was called up the next time the reading was finished in the ordinary desultory manner. A part of it had been read when it was called up finally for action. As will appear by the proceedings here the Senate was very attentive and full, and every amendment reported by the committee was thoroughly discussed and understood and explained. ` When the Senate came to section 15 of the bill after discussion it was stricken out. Section 16 of the House bill contained a silver dollar the equivalent of the 5-franc piece, but limited as a legal tender to $5.

The committee reported the following substitute for section 16:

The silver coins of the United States shall be a trade dollar, a half-dollar, or 50-cent piece, a quarter-dollar, or 25-cent piece, a dime, or 10-cent piece; and the weight of the trade dollar shall be 420 grains troy, the weight of the half-dollar shall be 12 grams and one-half of a gram, the quarter-dollar and the dime shall be, respectively, one-half and one-fifth of the weight of said half-dollar; and said coins shall be a legal tender at their nominal value for any amount not exceeding $5 in any one payment.

This substitute is now in the law, but it does not appear from the Globe that it was ever read or acted upon in the Senate. This is a strange omission. It is not probable that it has a parallel in the history of legislation. The usual mode of procedure in the Senate, where amendments have been proposed by committees, is to take them up seriatim, read and record them, and record the action thereon; after which the Presiding Officer will direct the Clerk to report the next amendment, and so on, until the amendments of the committee are disposed of.

This course was pursued without a variation in the passage of the bill under consideration, with the single exception of the substitute for section 16. In this case, after section 15 was read, discussed, and stricken out, the Clerk, instead of reading the substitute for section 16, proceeded to read the amendments to section 17. It may always remain a mystery whether this omission occurred by accident or design. This mystery has never been explained. When section 19 was reached, an important amendment was proposed, which is as follows:

"SEC. [19] 18. That upon the coins of the United States there shall be the following devices and legends: Upon one side there shall be an impression emblematic of liberty, with an inscription of the word "Liberty" and the year of the coinage, and upon the reverse shall be the figure or representation of an eagle, with the inscriptions "United States of America" and "E Pluribus Unum," and a designation of the value of the coin; but on the gold dollar and three-dollar piece, the silver dollar, half-dollar, quarter-dollar, the dime, five, three, and one cent piece the figure of the eagle shall be omitted, and on the reverse side of the silver dollar, half-dollar, quarter-dollar, and the dime, respectively, there shall be inscribed the weight and fineness of the coin; and the Director of the Mint, with the approval of the Secretary of the Treasury, may cause the motto "In God we trust" to be inscribed upon such coins as shall admit of such motto; and any one of the foregoing inscriptions may be on the rim of the gold and silver coins."

Mark, we had passed section 16, and if the amendment had been adopted there would have been no dollar in the bill on which to put a superscription. When this amendment was proposed, the Senator from California, who was a very careful man, always observing matters of a scientific nature, his mind running that way——

Mr. GEORGE. Who was he?

Mr. STEWART. Mr. Casserly, a very learned man, who knew

a good deal about the coin and currency, and he was a very accurate man in all his expressions. Mr. Casserly said:

I ask the Senator whether he is very strenuous in his advocacy of this amendment? I should like to save the American eagle on the half-dollar and quarter-dollar.
Mr. SHERMAN. The eagle is preserved on all the gold coins in a size large enough to be caged. [Laughter.]
Mr. CASSERLY. But the half-dollar and quarter-dollar are the money of the people and they are the leading coins of our entire silver coinage. I do not think it is of so much importance to put the fineness of the weight upon a half-dollar or a quarter-dollar as it might be upon a gold coin. I have never seen any foreign coin, and of course no American coin, marked in that way. To have the weight of the coin upon gold coin may be a useful thing because of the great preciousness of the metal; but what is the importance of having the weight inscribed upon the half-dollar or quarter-dollar? Does anybody ever weigh half-dollars or quarter-dollars in business?
Mr. SHERMAN. If the Senator will allow me, he will see that the preceding section provides for coin which is exactly interchangeable with the English shilling and the 5-franc piece of France; that is, a 5-franc piece of France will be the exact equivalent of a dollar of the United States in our silver coinage; and in order to show this wherever our silver coin shall float—and we are providing that it shall float all over the world—we propose to stamp upon it, instead of our eagle, which foreigners may not understand, and which they may not distinguish from a buzzard or some other bird, the intrinsic fineness and weight of the coin. In this practical, utilitarian age the officers of the Mint seemed to think it would be better to do that than to put the eagle on our silver coins.

Mr. SHERMAN'S remark that there was in the preceding section a silver dollar the exact equivalent of the 5-franc piece, was true as applied to the original section of the House bill, but was not true as applied to the substitute, which became a law. There was no such dollar in the substitute, as described by Mr. SHERMAN in his remarks above quoted, to float all over the world or to float at all. On the contrary, if the mysterious substitute had been adopted, the preceding section contained a trade dollar, not a dollar the exact equivalent of the 5-franc piece, as alleged by him. No discussion occurred at any time in the Senate on either of the mint bills with reference to the omission of the standard dollar from the list of coins.

The debate between Mr. Casserly and Mr. SHERMAN (a portion of which is quoted above) with regard to the superscription on our silver coins is all the discussion which took place on that subject. The Senate was satisfied with the explanation of Mr. SHERMAN and passed the bill without a division, on his assurance that it contained a silver dollar the exact equivalent of the 5-franc piece to float all over the world. The bill then went to a conference committee. The report of that committee referred to the amendments by numbers and did not call attention to the fact that the silver dollar was omitted from the list of coins. That conference report is as follows:

CONFERENCE REPORT.

IN SENATE, *Thursday, February 6, 1873.*

MINT LAWS.

Mr. SHERMAN submitted the following report:
The committee of conference on the disagreeing votes of the two Houses on the bill (H. R. 2934) revising and amending the laws relative to the mints and assay offices and coinage of the United States, having met, after full and free conference have agreed to recommend and do recommend to their respective Houses as follows:
That the House recede from its disagreement to the amendments of the Senate numbered 1, 2, 3, 5, 7, 10, 11, 13, 14, 15, 16, 17, 18, and 20; and agree to the same.

That the Senate recede from its fourth amendment, and agree to the words proposed to be stricken out, with the following amendments: After the word " by," in line 16, insert "natural;" in lines 17 and 18 strike out the words "on the double-eagle and eagle, and 1 per cent on the other coins;" and in line 19, after "law," insert the words "after a circulation of twenty years, as shown by its date of coinage, and at a ratable proportion for any period less than twenty years;" and the House agree to the same.

That the House recede from its disagreement to the sixth amendment of the Senate and agree to the same with the following amendments: In line 5 strike out the word "grains" at the end of the line, and insert in lieu thereof "grams (grammes;") and in line 6 strike out "grain" and insert "gram (gramme;") and the Senate agree to the same.

That the House recede from its disagreement to the eighth amendment of the Senate, and agree to the same with the following amendments: After "silver" insert "trade," strike out the words "half-dollar, quarter-dollar, and the dime, respectively, there shall be inscribed," and the word "the" before "fineness;" and after "coin," at the end of the amendment, insert the words "shall be inscribed;" and the Senate agree to the same.

That the House recede from its disagreement to the ninth amendment of the Senate and agree to the same with an amendment, as follows: Strike out the words proposed to be inserted, together with the remainder of the section, and in lieu thereof insert the following: "that any owner of silver bullion may deposit the same at any mint to be formed into bars or into dollars of the weight of 420 grains troy, designated in this act as trade dollars, and no deposit of silver for other coinage shall be received, but silver bullion contained in gold deposits and separated therefrom may be paid for in silver coin at such valuation as may be from time to time established by the Director of the Mint;" and the Senate agree to the same.

That the House recede from its disagreement to the twelfth amendment of the Senate, and agree to the same with amendments as follows; Strike out the words proposed to be inserted and insert after "for," in line 3, section 26, the words "converting standard silver into trade-dollars, for melting and;" and in line 3, strike out "the;" and the Senate agree to the same.

That the House recede from its disagreement to the nineteenth amendment of the Senate, and agree to the same with an amendment as follows: Insert after "New York." in line 8, page 36 of the bill, the words "the United States assay office at Charlotte, N. C.;" and the Senate agree to the same.

JOHN SHERMAN,
JOHN SCOTT,
T. F. BAYARD,
Managers on the part of the Senate.
S. HOOPER,
WM. M. STOUGHTON,
Managers on the part of the House.

The report was concurred in.—(*Congressional Globe*, part 2, third session, Forty-second Congress, 1872-'73, page 1150.)

It will be perceived that the amendment is designated just by number, and no explanation was in the report, and the record shows no explanation to the Senate of the changes that had been made.

This was the legislation that the Senator from Ohio says was enacted on a petition from California, which statement I deny and demand proof. It is shown by the declarations of good and honest men that the demonetization of silver was a secret at the time, and if any man except the chairman of the committee knew how or when silver was demonetized, he has not confessed it in either House. I hold in my hand the evidence of a large number of gentlemen of the highest character who were in Congress at the time and took an active part in the affairs of legi lation, who state that they had no knowledge of the demonetization of silver, or of dropping the silver dollar from the list of coins. I will read part and furnish the rest in my remarks. I will read first what Senator Thurman said in a debate in the Senate February 15, 1878:

I can not say what took place in the House, but know when the bill was pending in the Senate we thought it was simply a bill to reform the Mint, regulate coinage, and fix up one thing and another, and there is not a single man in the Senate. I think, unless a member of the committee from which the bill came, who had the slightest idea that it was even a squint toward demonetization.—*Congressional Record*, volume 7, part 2, Forty-fifth Congress, second session, page 1034.

The others are equally strong, and the array of witnesses includes the first men in the nation, who had charge of the affairs of the country at that time. It seems to me that of the long list I have here some one would have known something about it, and that som·body would have come forward and said he knew when this great change took place. I will print the testimony of these men in my remarks. I shall not take the time of the Senate to read it.

Mr. Bright, of Tennessee, said of the law:

It passed by fraud in the House, never having been printed in advance, being a substitute for the printed bill; never having been read at the Clerk's desk, the reading having been dispensed with by an impression that the bill made no material alteration in the coinage laws; it was passed without discussion, debate being cut off by operation of the previous question. It was passed, to my certain information, under such circumstances that the fraud escaped the attention of some of the most watchful as well as the ablest statesmen in Congress at that time. * * * Aye, sir, it was a fraud that smells to heaven. It was a fraud that will stink in the nose of posterity, and for which some persons must give account in the day of retribution.—*Congressional Record*, volume 7, part 1, second session Forty-fifth Congress, page 584.

Mr. HOLMAN, in a speech delivered in the House of Representatives July 13, 1876, said:

I have before me the record of the proceedings of this House on the passage of that measure, a record which no man can read without being convinced that the measure and the method of its passage through this House was a "colossal swindle." I assert that the measure never had the sanction of this House, and it does not possess the moral force of law.—*Congressional Record*, volume 4, part 6, Forty-fourth Congress, first session, appendix, page 193.

Again on August 5, 1876, he said:

The original bill was simply a bill to organize a bureau of mines and coinage. The bill which finally passed the House and which ultimately became a law was certainly not read in this House.

* * * * * *

It was never considered before the House as it was passed, Up to the time the bill came before this House for final passage the measure had simply been one to establish a bureau of mines; I believe I use the term correctly now. It came from the Committee on Coinage, Weights, and Measures. The substitute which finally became a law was never read, and is subject to the charge made against it by the gentleman from Missouri [Mr. BLAND], that it was passed by the House without a knowledge of its provisions, especially upon that of coinage.

I myself asked the question of Mr. Hooper, who stood near where I am now standing, whether it changed the law in regard to coinage. And the answer of Mr. Hooper certainly left the impression upon the whole House that the subject of the coinage was not affected by that bill.—*Congressional Record*, volume 4, part 6, Forty-fourth Congress, first session, page 5237.

Mr. Cannon, of Illinois, in a speech made in the House on July 13, 1876, said:

This legislation was had in the Forty-second Congress, February 12, 1873, by a bill to regulate the mints of the United States, and practically abolished, silver as money by failing to provide for the coinage of the silver dollar. It was not discussed, as shown by the RECORD, and neither members of Congress nor the people understood the scope of the legislation.—*Ibid*, appendix, page 197.

Senator Bogy, of Missouri, uttered the following words in a speech made in the Senate June 27, 1876:

Why the act of 1873, which forbids the coinage of the silver dollar, was passed, no one at this day can give a good reason.—*Congressional Record*, volume 4, part 5, Forty-fourth Congress, first session, page 4173.

Mr. Burchard, of Illinois, in a speech made in the House of Representatives on July 13, 1876, said:

⌈The coinage act of 1873, unaccompanied by any written report upon the subject from any committee, and unknown to the members of Congress, who without opposition, allowed it to pass under the belief, if not assurance, that it made no alteration in the value of the current coins, changed the unit of value from silver to gold.—*Ibid.*, page 4560.

Senator Conkling, in the Senate on March 30, 1876, during the remarks of Senator Bogy on the bill (S. 263) to amend the laws relating to legal tender of silver coin, in surprise, inquired:

Will the Senator allow me to ask him or some other Senator a question? Is it true that there is now by law no American dollar? And, if so, is it true that the effect of this bill is to be to make half-dollars and quarter-dollars the only silver coin which can be used as a legal tender?—*Congressional Record*, volume 4, part 3, Forty-fourth Congress, first session, page 2032.

Gen. Garfield, in a speech made at Springfield, Ohio, during the fall of 1877, said:

Perhaps I ought to be ashamed to say so, but it is the truth to say that, I at that time being chairman of the Committee on Appropriations, and having my hands overfull during all that time with work, I never read the bill. I took it upon the faith of a prominent Democrat and a prominent Republican, and I do not know that I voted at all. There was no call of the yeas and nays, and nobody opposed that bill that I know of. It was put through as dozens of bills are, as my friend and I know, in Congress, on the faith of the report of the chairman of the committee; therefore I tell you, because it is the truth, that I have no knowledge about it.—*Congressional Record*, volume 7, part 1, Forty-fifth Congress, second session, page 989.

Senator ALLISON, on February 15, 1878, when the bill (H.R. 1093) to authorize the free coinage of the standard silver dollar and to restore its legal-tender character was under consideration, observed:

But when the secret history of this bill of 1873 comes to be told, it will disclose the fact that the House of Representatives intended to coin both gold and silver, and intended to place both metals upon the French relation instead of on our own, which was the true scientific position with reference to this subject in 1873, but that the bill afterward was doctored, if I may use that term, and I use it in no offensive sense of course——

Mr. Sargent interrupted him and asked him what he meant by the word "doctored."

Mr. ALLISON said:

I said I used the word in no offensive sense. It was changed after discussion, and the dollar of 420 grains was substituted for it.—*Congressional Record*, volume 7, part 2, Forty-fifth Congress, second session, page 1038.

On February 15, 1878, during the consideration of the bill above referred to, the following colloquy between Senator Blaine and Senator VOORHEES took place:

Mr. VOORHEES. I want to ask my friend from Maine, whom I am glad to designate in that way, whether I may call him as one more witness to the fact that it was not generally known whether silver was demonetized. Did he know, as Speaker of the House, presiding at that time, that the silver dollar was demonetized in the bill to which he alludes?

Mr. BLAINE. I did not know anything that was in the bill at all. As I have before said, little was known or cared on the subject. [Laughter.] And now I should like to exchange questions with the Senator from Indiana, who was then on the floor and whose business it was, far more than mine, to know, because by the designation of the House I was to put questions; the Senator from Indiana, then on the floor of the House, with his power as a debater, was to unfold them to the House. Did he know?

Mr. VOORHEES. I very frankly say that I did not.—*Ibid.*, page 1063.

Senator Beck, in a speech made in the Senate January 10, 1878, said:

It [the bill demonetizing silver] never was understood by either House of Congress. I say that with full knowledge of the facts. No newspaper re-

porter—and they are the most vigilant men I ever saw in obtaining information—discovered that it had been done.—*Congressional Record*, volume 7, part
1, Forty-fifth Congress, second session, page 260.

Senator Hereford, in the Senate, on February 13, 1878, in discussing the demonetization of silver, said:

So that I say that beyond the possibility of a doubt—and there is no dis-
puting it—that bill which demonetized silver, as it passed, never was read,
never was discussed, and that the chairman of the committee who reported
it, who offered the substitute, said to Mr. HOLMAN, when inquired of, that it
did not affect the coinage in any way whatever.—*Ibid*, page 989.

Mr. Kelley, of Pennsylvania, who had charge of the bill, in a
speech made in the House of Representatives on March 9, 1878 said:

In connection with the charge that I advocated the bill which demonetized
the standard silver dollar, I say that, though the chairman of the Committee on
Coinage, I was ignorant of the fact that it would demonetize the silver dollar or of its dropping the silver dollar from our system of coins as were those
distinguished Senators Messrs. Blaine and VOORHEES, who were then members of the House, and each of whom a few days since interrogated the
other: "Did you know it was dropped when the bill passed?" "No,"
said Mr. Blaine; "did you?" "No," said Mr. VOORHEES. I do not think
that there were three members in the House that knew it. I doubt whether
Mr. Hooper, who, in my absence from the Committee on Coinage and attend-
ance on the Committee on Ways and Means, managed the bill, knew it. I
say this in justice to him.—*Congressional Record*, volume 7, part 2, Forty-
fifth Congress, second session, page 1605.

Again on May 10, 1879, Mr. Kelley said:

All I can say is that the Committee on Coinage, Weights, and Measures,
who reported the original bill, were faithful and able, and scanned its provisions closely; that as their organ I reported it; that it contained provision
for both the standard silver dollar and the trade-dollar. Never having heard
until a long time after its enactment into law of the substitution in the
Senate of the section which dropped the standard dollar, I profess to know
nothing of its history; but I am prepared to say that in all the legislation
of this country there is no mystery equal to the demonetization of the standard silver dollar of the United States. I have never found a man who could
tell just how it came about or why.—*Congressional Record*, volume 9, part 1,
Forty-sixth Congress, first session, page 1231.

Senator Howe, in a speech delivered in the Senate on February 5, 1878, said:

Mr. President, I do not regard the demonetization of silver as an attempt
to wrench from the people more than they agreed to pay. That is not the
crime of which I accuse the act of 1873. I charge it with guilt compared with
which the robbery of two hundred millions is venial.—*Congressional Record*,
volume 7, part 1, Forty-fifth Congress, second session, page 764.

President Grant was also ignorant of the demonetization of silver. Eight months after the passage of the bill he wrote a letter
to Mr. Cowdrey, from which the following extract is taken:

The panic has brought greenbacks about to a par with silver. I wonder that
silver is not already coming into the market to supply the deficiency in the
circulating medium. When it does come, and I predict that it will soon, we
will have made a rapid stride towards specie payments. Currency will never
go below silver after that. The circulation of silver will have other bene-
ficial effects. Exp'rience has proved that it takes about forty millions of
fractional currency to make small change necessary for the transaction of
the business of the country. Silver will gradually take the place of this
currency, and, further, will become the standard of values which will be
hoarded in a small way. I estimate that this will consume from two to
three hundred millions, in time, of this species of our circulating medium.
It will leave the paper currency free to perform the legitimate functions
of trade and will tend to bring us back where we must come at last, to a
specie basis. I confess to a desire to see a limited hoarding of money. It
insures a firm foundation in time of need. But I want to see the hoarding
of something that has a standard of value the world over. Silver has this,
and if we once get back to that our strides toward a higher appreciation of
our currency will be rapid. Our mines are now producing almost unlimited
amounts of silver, and it is becoming a question, "What shall we do with

it?" I suggest here a solution that will answer for some years, and suggest to you bankers whether you may not imitate it: To put it in circulation now; keep it there until it is fixed, and then we will find other markets.— *McPherson's Handbook of Politics for 1874, pages 134 and 135.*

I have disposed of the question of ratio. I have shown that if the ratio is changed at all on the theory of production the quantity of gold in the gold dollar should be increased, and not the quantity of silver in the silver dollar. J have shown that when silver was produced at the rate of 69 to 31, 31 of gold to 69 of silver, the ratio of 15½ to 1 was sustained without a break, and that notwithstanding for over three hundred years the ratio of production had been 31 of gold to 69 of silver, the mint ratio had never risen above 15¼ to 1.

Mr. GEORGE. Is that in ounces or parts?

Mr. STEWART. In money, in par value, 15½ ounces, taking the money value at the ratio of 15½ to 1. Since 1850 we find that of the two metals, on the ratio of the coinage value at 16 to 1 in this country, the entire production of the world has been 40 of silver to 60 of gold. So I have shown that it was not the ratio of production which reduced the price of silver.

Mr. GEORGE. Is that the ratio now?

Mr. STEWART. No; there has been a little more silver than gold produced in the past year or two. It may not be permanent. But I am taking the average ratio for the last forty years. We must take it for some period. By taking a single year we can not fix it. I do not know what the ratio now is. I dislike to state the figures in regard to production recently; there has been so much speculation in the whole business; but I think the entire production of both gold and silver is very much exaggerated. I have little faith in recent statistics for the reason that all the mines of the world are on the market, and the disposition to exaggerate the output is very great, particularly in Spanish American countries, where we have no means of getting very accurate statistics. The accounts of the production of silver I have no doubt are misleading. It may not be so, but I can not question it, because no man can look it up for himself.

The Senator from Ohio reads from the statement of some person in a San Francisco paper saying that the United States is going to produce $100,000,000 of silver a year. We have heard from a fellow-Senator that we are going to quintuple the production of that metal. I tell you that an increased production of silver is difficult. It costs in labor of exploration and development two or three times as much as it does in mining. Every ounce of silver must cost from two to four or five dollars. Probably $4 would be a fair value for every ounce of silver, if you count the entire exploration that leads up to it.

Mr. GEORGE. Then why do they mine it?

Mr. STEWART. Men mine it because occasionally a great mine is opened. If it had not been for accidental finds there would have been no gold and silver mining, taking into account the losses, but when there is such an enormous gain when a find is made, the people will endure the loss. That is why mining is carried on at all. The absurdity of estimating the cost of production of silver by the expenses of mining a bonanza when found is annoying to those familiar with the subject. It is like estimating the cost of the production of wheat by the expense of taking it to market. Bonanzas, when found, sell for vast sums of money, but the dreary work of sinking shafts, running tunnels, and climbing over mountains and precipices to find them are a necessary part of the cost of production.

In this connection let me say that the miners by this act of the Senator from Ohio—for it was his act—have suffered in actual discount more than $150,000,000. Over $80,000,000 of that has gone into the Treasury as royalty. The Senator says if it was exacted from the people as a royalty it would be the greatest outrage on earth. What else is it?

It was the discovery of mines that laid the foundation of our financial prosperity. Previous to 1850 the whole world was laboring under the dark cloud of contraction, stagnation, and hard times. The wages of labor were at a starvation point and enterprises were checked for want of money. But when the flood of gold came from California and Australia it breathed new life into all the channels of commerce throughout the world. It gave men new courage, and development went on, riches were acquired, and an era of prosperity for twenty-five years followed the like of which the world has never seen.

The advance of civilization during the first twenty-five years, from 1850 to 1875, surpasses that of any hundred years in the history of the world. The flood of the precious metals came and it came violently. Do you talk about a flood of silver now? The product of gold from 1848 to 1852 rose from a nominal amount of not more than fifteen or twenty million dollars per annum to $196,000,000 in 1852. Did the world suffer by it? If there had been such a flood of silver as that there might be an outcry about it; there might be some danger; but, on the contrary, did not all mankind prosper, was it not the greatest boon that ever happened to the human race, and has there been anything since to check that boon but the act of 1873? The supply of the two metals combined has been more uniform since 1850 until now than at any other time in the history of man. The increase has been gradual. It has been enough to keep pace with the growth of population and business; but what a boon it would be if it had all gone into the channels of commerce and sustained their credit.

(At this point the honorable Senator yielded to a motion to adjourn.)

Thursday, June 2, 1892.

Mr. STEWART. Mr. President, I was somewhat surprised day before yesterday at the remarks of the Senator from Ohio [Mr. SHERMAN] wherein he expressed his admiration of the Bland bill in the following manner, in answer to a question by the Senator from Colorado [Mr. TELLER]:

Mr. TELLER. I should like to know of the Senator, if he will answer the question, whether he was in favor of what he called the Bland-Allison act?
Mr. SHERMAN. I think I have answered that once or twice, Mr. President. I was opposed to the Bland bill, though not then a member of Congress, but Secretary of the Treasury, and so stated in a public speech. Does the Senator wish me to repeat it? I stated in a public speech in the Senate and on the stump that I was opposed to the Bland bill. but I was in favor of the Allison bill; that I did not concur in the view taken by President Hayes as to the Allison bill, because I drew a clear line of distinction between the Allison bill and the Bland bill. One was for the free coinage of silver and

the other was for the purpose of establishing a bimetallic standard of gold
and silver tied to each other.

Mr. TELLER. The Senator does not answer my question. I did not ask
him if he was in favor of the Bland bill; I asked him if he was in favor of the
Bland-Allison bill.

Mr. SHERMAN. There is no Bland-Allison bill. They took all the Bland out
of it when they put the Allison in it. [Laughter.]

Mr. TELLER. I wish very much the Senator from Ohio would answer the
question whether he was in favor of the bill of February 28, 1878.

Mr. SHERMAN. I was in favor of what I call the Allison bill. The Senator
from Colorado can not compel me to give a bad name to a good measure.
[Laughter.]

I say I was surprised at these remarks in view of my familiar-
ity with the history of the views expressed by the Senator from
Ohio upon that very subject while he was Secretary of the Treasury. In three elaborate reports, made in 1878, 1879, and 1880, he
discussed the Bland bill, as he called it, and used precisely the
same arguments with regard to it that he does with regard to
the bill now under consideration. He made the same prediction,
and if I were to read these various reports at length it would be
difficult to distinguish them from the speech delivered in the
last two days by him. I will ask to be indulged to read a portion. I read now from his first report on the subject, which was
in 1878-'79. He said:

When the resumption act passed, gold was the only coin which by law was
a legal tender in payment of all debts. That act contemplated resumption
in gold coin only. No silver coin of full legal tender could then be lawfully
issued. The only silver coin provided was fractional coin, which was a legal
tender for $5 only. The act approved February 28, 1878, made a very impor-
tant change in our coinage system. The silver dollar provided for was made
a legal tender for debts, public and private, except where otherwise ex-
pressly stipulated in the contract. The amount of this coin issued will more
properly be stated hereafter, but its effect upon the problem of resumption
should be here considered.

The law itself clearly shows that the silver dollar was not to supersede
the gold dollar; nor did Congress propose to adopt the single standard of
silver, but only to create a bimetallic standard of silver and gold, of equal
value and equal purchasing power. Congress, therefore, limited the amount
of silver dollars to be coined to not less than two millions nor more than
four millions per month, but did not limit the aggregate amount nor the
period of time during which this coinage should continue. The market
value of the silver in the dollar at the date of the passage of the act was
93½ cents in gold coin. Now it is about 86 cents in gold coin. If it was intended by Congress to adopt the silver instead of the gold standard, the
amount provided for is totally inadequate for the purpose. Experience, not
only in this country, but in European countries, has established that a certain amount of silver coin may be maintained in circulation at par with
gold, though of less intrinsic bullion value.

It was, no doubt, the intention of Congress to provide a coin in silver which
would answer a multitude of the purposes of business life, without banish-
ing from circulation the established gold coin of the country. To accomplish this it is indispensable either that the silver coin be limited in amount,
or that its bullion value be equal to that of the gold dollar. If not, its use
will be limited to domestic purposes. It can not be exported except at its
commercial value as bullion. If issued in excess of demands for domestic
purposes, it will necessarily fall in market value, and, by a well-known princi-
ple of finance, will become the sole coin standard of value. Gold will be either
hoarded or exported. When two currencies, both legal, are authorized without limit, the cheaper alone will circulate. If, however, the issue of the silver
dollars is limited to an amount demanded for circulation, there will be no
depreciation, and their convenient use will keep them at par with gold, as
fractional silver coin, issued under the act approved February 21, 1853, was
kept at par with gold—*House Executive Document No. 2*, Forty-fifth Congress,
third session, page 14.

He goes on and discusses it at length, using the same argument that he does now against free coinage, and he finally said:

It would, therefore, seem to be the best policy for the present to limit the
aggregate issue of our silver dollars, based on the ratio of 16 to 1, to such

515

sums as can clearly be maintained at par with gold, until the price of silver in the market shall assume a definite ratio to gold, when that ratio should be adopted, and our coins made to conform to it; and the Secretary respectfully recommends that he be authorized to discontinue the coinage of the silver dollar when the amount outstanding shall exceed $50,000,000—*Ibid.*, page 17.

This was in the same year that the act was passed. Still the Senator informs us that he did not agree with Mr. Hayes's veto. Then at the next session he quotes the last paragraph which I have read. He repeats it and urges action upon Congress to suspend the coinage, and he further says:

It is impossible to ascertain what amount of silver coin, based upon the ratio of 16 of silver to 1 of gold, can be maintained at par with gold, but it is manifest that this can only be done by the Government holding in its vaults the great body of the silver coin. It would seem that nothing would be gained by an unlimited coinage unless it is desirable to measure all values by the silver standard. The Secretary can not too strongly urge the importance of adjusting the coinage ratio of the two metals by treaties with commercial nations, and, until this can be done, of limiting the coinage of the silver dollar to such a sum as, in the opinion of Congress, would enable the Department to readily maintain the standard dollars of gold and silver at par with each other.—*House Executive Document No 2*, Forty-sixth Congress, second session, page 14.

He did not think it was a very good bill, it seems to me. These recommendations continued as long as he was Secretary of the Treasury. I read last from the report of 1879-'80, on page 14. Then again, in 1880-'81, he goes over the arguments at length, reiterates them, and urges suspension of the act; and among other things he said:

For these reasons the Secretary respectfully but earnestly recommends that the further compulsory coinage of the silver dollar be suspended, or, as an alternative, that the number of grains of silver in the dollar be increased so as to make it equal in market value to the gold dollar, and that its coinage be left as other coinage to the Secretary of the Treasury or the Director of the Mint, to depend upon the demand for it by the public for convenient circulation.—*House Executive Document No. 2*, Forty-sixth Congress, third session, page 19.

After having in three elaborate reports, too lengthy to be read, criticised the bill and demanded its repeal in the most urgent manner, we are told that it was a good bill and he approved it and differed with the President who vetoed it. It seems to me that his recollection upon this subject must be very defective or his prophecies and his predictions are not very valuable. He tells us that free coinage will bring us to a silver standard just as he predicted the Bland act would do.

Now, our present law will do worse than that. The present law on the statute book which he approves to-day (he may not approve it to-morrow) will do worse than that. It will inevitably bring us to a paper standard or the market-value standard of silver, because it is going to be utterly impossible—there is no use in deceiving ourselves upon this subject—to maintain gold payments under existing laws.

We have outstanding nearly $1,000,000,000 of paper. We have in the Treasury, of gold, if silver is rejected, only $118,000,000 which can be used to redeem that paper, according to the last statement, and according to a statement I saw in the papers yesterday it is now reduced to $113,000,000. This includes the $100,-000,000 that has been regarded as a reserve for the redemption of greenbacks. Every monthly and every weekly statement that comes out shows that the amount of gold going into the Treasury is less and less per cent. The gold receipts have dwindled down to only 14 per cent of the revenues of the United States.

But I noticed an interview with the Secretary of the Treasury and the promise he made on yesterday, which there is no law to carry out and which the country never will tolerate. I read from the Press, of New York, of June 2, 1892:

NO PREMIUM ON GOLD NOW—SECRETARY FOSTER PROPOSES TO CONTINUE THE PARITY OF SILVER.

Secretary Foster had a busy day in Wall street yesterday. A number of bankers called upon him at the subtreasury and discussed finances. In regard to increasing the supply of gold in the National Treasury, Mr. Foster said:

"I do not care to say anything on that subject now. If I intended to take any action it would be very poor policy to talk about it. There is one thing, however, of which every one may be sure, and that is that there will be no premium on gold during this Administration. I have the power to issue bonds to keep the two metals at a parity, and they will be kept at a parity."

The threat is to sell bonds and buy gold to keep these metals at a parity and to redeem our paper and silver in gold. Silver as well as the paper is to be treated by the Department as credit money to rest on gold alone. It is idle to talk about the silver in the Treasury. It can play no part as money of ultimate redemption as long as it is treated as credit money, as a commodity, and not as a basis of credit to sustain the fabric of credit.

As I said before, it will be impossible to maintain the gold standard under the present law on the theory of the Administration. It is true Congress might authorize the Treasury constantly to buy gold. It would require hundreds of millions each year. We might sell bonds and buy gold, but are we willing to involve the country in a large national debt for the purpose of destroying silver and enriching a few who have a corner on gold? Are the people prepared for that?

That is the broad proposition, to sell bonds and buy gold, and the more gold you buy the more you will have to pay for it, the cheaper your commodities will be, the harder it will be to pay your debt. Gold will go up. This plan of compelling the world to compete for gold has already enhanced the price of gold nearly 100 per cent. It has about doubled its purchasing power. The United States has been buying gold to pay debts contracted to be paid in greenbacks or silver. What has been the result? The farmers and producers have had to discount their property. They had to sell it in the European markets to buy gold. What has been the result? Let the price of wheat and cotton answer the question. That price is continually declining as gold goes up.

Mr. HIGGINS. Will the Senator yield to a question?

Mr. STEWART. Yes, if it is a question.

Mr. HIGGINS. It is a question. I ask the Senator if, instead of the maintenance of the gold reserved by the purchase of bonds, he would prefer under existing law that the country should come to a silver basis? I understood the Senator just now to prophesy that we could not maintain gold payments, and I assume if we can not maintain gold payments we must come to a silver basis. My question is whether he would prefer that, if that is his argument?

Mr. STEWART. I would prefer the country to do anything rather than have it enslave the people by attempting to reduce the whole world to the narrow basis of gold. What does the gold standard mean? Three billion seven hundred million dollars is all the real money that exists for the entire world. All the other money is credit money. It means wages put down, the price of property decreased, the people enslaved to buy gold to pay obligations contracted in silver or paper, and as they bring other nations in and compel them to buy gold they put down the price of property and enrich those who have a corner on gold.

Nothing could be as bad as that. I would use the silver in the Treasury for redemption as provided by law. There is $500,-000,000 of silver coin in the country. Over $400,000,000 of it is in the Treasury, and the law makes it a legal tender equally with gold. I would reverse the policy of the Administration, which is in violation of law. From the beginning the law at all times gave to the Government the option to pay its obligations in either gold or silver. There never was a gold obligation of the Government. At all events there has not been for the last twenty years a gold obligation of the Government, and it is the duty of the Secretary of the Treasury to redeem the paper of the Government in that currency which is most convenient. I say the present policy under existing law will not only reduce us to a silver basis, but lower our basis to the commercial price of silver. The proposal to sell bonds and buy gold will not be tolerated.

It is impossible upon the present volume of gold to maintain the existing fabric of credit in the world. Eighteen years ago there was not more than 60 per cent as much indebtedness as there is to-day, and I do not think there was more than 50 per cent. There was then under that credit $7,500,000,000 or $7,800,-000,000 of gold and silver coin, which the Royal Commission of England said was one money. Nobody thought it was too much to sustain the credit of the world and the paper circulation. No suggestion of that kind was ever made. It was not too much. But now you have 30 to 50 per cent more credit, more business, more people, and you have only half as much money of ultimate payment with which to redeem it. You have only $3,700,000,000 of gold coin in the world.

Mr. PEFFER. Mr. President——

The PRESIDING OFFICER (Mr. DIXON in the chair). Does the Senator from Nevada yield to the Senator from Kansas?

Mr. STEWART. Certainly.

Mr. PEFFER. I should like to inquire of the Senator if, as is assumed, we are now on a gold basis whether we should be able to pay our debts in gold to-day, and if not, what proportion we could pay in gold?

Mr. STEWART. The world is bankrupt on a gold basis. The failure of the Barings disclosed the fact, which I had stated exist-d for years, that there was not gold enough, and because of that failure the chancellor of the exchequer, in a public speech, told the bankers of Great Britain that they must increase their gold and reduce their credit or they would be bankrupted.

Since silver was demonetized more than $1,500,000,000 of silver has been discarded and its place supplied with gold for reserves. How long can this continue? The gold kings tell us it must continue until all the world is compelled to do business on $3,700,000,000 of gold. The Senator from Ohio said that the financial condition of the world was such that we ought not to discuss it; that it ought to be discussed only by wise men; that we are creating a panic by discussing it. What! Is our financial system so rotten that it will not bear discussion? That is what he is telling us. Why should the financial condition of the world be so rotton, so sensitive, if not because its vast credit rests upon only $3,700,000,000 of gold? Roumania and Belgium are to be brought in; and some say they will bring India into the combination and make her sell her $900,000,000 of silver and replace it with gold. This threat is made when all the world is trembling on the brink of bankruptcy on account of want of a sufficient basis.

There is not gold enough. The Secretary of the Treasury said on the 17th of December last to the bankers of New York at Delmonico's that it is conceded that there is not gold enough. Still he would not increase the metallic basis by the use of silver as money.

Mr. SHERMAN tells us it is bimetallism to coin silver and keep it at a parity with gold, by a promise of redemption in gold. Why use silver if it depends on gold for its value? How does it add to the volume of money of ultimate payment? Why is it not credit money as much as paper? You do not remedy the difficulty by using silver as credit money. So far as we know since prehistoric times people have valued silver for its money function. Take the money function away and your security is gone. The fabric of credit is trembling, and the Secretary of the Treasury tells the people in New York he will, in violation of law, sell bonds and buy gold rather than treat silver as money. No political party dare do it. It would bring untold misery upon the people of the United States.

If you buy gold you must sell your commodities to obtain it. This we have done until our resources are sadly impaired. Why is there no money for use in the country districts? It is because the gold kings know full well that no man engaged in productive industry can now afford to borrow and pay gold. They know it can not be done. Nothing is good for security except collaterals that can be immediately converted. Gold goes to the centers. They dare not put it out because they know it can not return, and a promise to pay in gold would be futile. It would be like the United States promising to deliver that which did not exist. Credit is nothing unless it is possible to obtain the article promised, and that is impossible in this struggle.

The Senator from Ohio continues to boast of the prosperity of the country. It is true our resources and practical enterprises are greater; our people are more energetic; they are not so much depressed as the people are in Europe; their wages go down there, but there the strong arm of the military prevents discussion. In Germany they fire upon labor organizations before they order them to disperse. Does not that mean slavery? And how long will it be before the people of this country, like all the rest of the world, being deprived of money, will become docile, weak, and pusillanimous?

The old Romans were as brave a people as we are, and when they lost their money they submitted to slavery, and not till then. This money trust understand this matter, and they use their power in every hamlet. Every man who is in debt gets notice that he must pay. Why, the people of this country stand in more dread of this money power than the serfs of Russia ever felt for their august monarch.

This money trust has the public press. They will nominate their men at our conventions. They tell us that those who want to fight over the tariff schedule can have the privilege. Just so much money for the expenses of the Government, $500,000,000 a year, is needed, and we must have that amount of money. The people will not submit to direct taxation. Consequently we have a sure thing; we will let you fight about the schedules. That is all we care about. So argues the gold trust, Talk about tariff reform! Tariff reform is only a controversy about schedules! It is a good big phrase, but what do they mean by it? What do they mean by tariff reform? We have civil-service reform and . a whole lot of reforms and shams. That is what we may fight over. That is what is presented for discussion in the present financial crisis.

The present financial condition is such, according to the Senator from Ohio, the leader of the gold trust, the inventor of this device to destroy the world's money, that the representatives of the people must not discuss the question; that it will do harm.

I tell you it is best now to know the worst before it shall be too late. What is the reason for our present condition? Why should it be so? Has anything in nature occurred that should make this disturbance in the financial condition of the world?

In this country we went through a serious depression from 1810 to 1850, on account of the lack of precious metals. Those were gloomy times. But now we have no such thing. From 1850 to the present time there has been a reasonable amount of the precious metals produced, sufficient to place the world on a sound financial basis. If the coining of the precious metals had not been tampered with there would have been good times.

Why should the world be trembling on the brink of bankruptcy? Why should the subject be too delicate for discussion? We have had profound peace ever since the war, twenty-seven years ago. The mines have yielded bountifully. and nothing but the contrivances of man has brought us into this condition. I say it was because of the passage of the act of 1873.

The S·nator undertakes to say that the. paper we are now issuing in exchange for silver is in some way made secure by silver in the Treasury. That is all a mistake. What security would silver be if it is not used as money? Suppose we were to sell it; would it sell for $2 a pound? Nobody needs it if it can not be used as money, if it can not be made the basis of credit. Its exclusion from the mint destroys its money function, without which it is no security.

Besides, the Senator says that behind the money issued under the act of 1890 there is a dollar of silver for every dollar so issued. The act declares that the paper issued under it is redeemable in gold or silver coin, and makes it the duty of the Secretary to coin silver for the purposes of redemption, and provides no other redemption but coin. The act furnishes a coin redemption, not a bullion redemption.

The talk about its being secured by anything but silver dollars when there are no gold dollars to pay out is utter nonsense,

515——3

and is an att mpt to deceive the people. It is the duty under that act of the Secretary of the Treasury to coin silver dollars, and make all Government payments with them when it is necessary. But his refusal to do that and his threat to sell bonds with which to buy gold are calculated to precipitate a crisis. Such an attempt will dishonor the Government, and it can not be done.

Bimetallism, the Senator says, is the two metals kept on a parity by the credit of the Government. What is the use of silver under that state of things? If the precious metals can not keep themselves at a parity we do not want them as money, and there is no use for them. The credit of the Government! We can have that without using silver at all, and if that is the reason for the purchase of silver, its purchase is an arrant humbug and a wasteful extravagance. There is no excuse for its purchase unless it is to use it as real money, as a foundation to support this vast fabric of credit. If you do not put this foundation under the structure of credit it will fall.

The Senator also says he is no more opposed to silver than to any other commodity. I do not suppose he has any personal hate against silver. I do not know how a man could have any particular prejudice against a particular kind of metal. But he wants it used as a commodity. It is now used by the Administration as a commodity. There is more than a hundred years' supply on hand for other purposes besides money, perhaps a two hundred years' supply of it as a commodity. If it is not to be a part of the basis then it is of no use whatever.

He says we propose a new standard. We do not propose a new standard. We ask a return to the ancient standard, the standard that was maintained from the foundation of the Government until the act of 1873. That is all we ask. We ask to place under our paper the silver dollars of standard value. We ask the Treasury Department to use them now as money.

Then the Senator says we never had, in the true sense of the word, free coinage of silver. All we ask to be given to us is that which we had from the foundation of the Government, when a man could take silver to the Mint and have it coined into full legal-tender money. That is all we ask. That is why gold is valuable, because it has access to the mints. But if you treat gold as you have treated silver, you will destroy it. How absurd to call this rejection of silver the policy of the fathers. All we ask is to restore silver to the position it occupied before the crime of 1873, then we will have the policy of the fathers.

But the Senator says it has been the policy of this Government for the last thirty years to have tentative legislation, experimental legislation. I am tired of these new inventions. I want to be supported by the experience of mankind. I prefer it to the experience of the Senator from Ohio or any of his associates. His experiments are a very unreliable standard on which to do business. The fathers made no experiments of this kind. We want no more of them.

He says free coinage of silver in every country of the world expels gold. Is that true? Was gold expelled from France or from any bimetallic country while silver was coined equally with it?

Then he refers us to Mexico as an example. I tell you Mexico is a good example. The people of that country have a better financial system than we have, and they are prospering; and, other things being equal, they can manufacture in Mexico about 25 per cent cheaper than we can in this country, and that is because they have plenty of good money. They could not have stood the burdens they have stood if they had not had plenty of good money.

Then the Senator also refers us to the Argentine Confederation and Brazil as examples of the free coinage of silver. That is a good illustration. You will remember that in the early part of 1890, along in January and February, there was some trouble in these countries, and a commission of Englishmen was sent there to settle it. It was published in the papers that they had put these countries on a gold basis, changing the obligations to gold. I said then in a public speech that that meant repudiation; that they could not get the gold. In about six months, when the first interest came due, the whole bubble collapsed. They had agreed to do something that they could not do. That was what ailed those countries. They had undertaken to pay what they could not pay. These smart Englishmen who went there and put those countries on a gold basis sowed the wind, and they reaped the whirlwind. That is what the whole world will do if it continues to attempt to maintain this fabric of credit on a gold basis.

Then the Senator from Ohio refers us to India. I have read the same papers that he quoted from. I am familiar with them and have read both sides all the time. I know the situation there and what the controversy is, I believe, as well as one can know it from the discussions before the Royal Commission, in the public press, and the discussions that were had last fall, which were very important, in Birmingham, by the Textile Fabric Association and some of the labor organizations, in regard to manufacturing. It was stated that the depreciation of silver is very damaging to the finances of India, which are payable in gold in London. It has added to them about 33½ per cent and it is crushing them. That was stated over and over again before the Royal Commission. It also operated heavily upon English officeholders in India, who are paid in rupees and who have to import clothing, luxuries, etc. Their salaries are diminished more than 33½ per cent and they have been making a very loud noise for a very long time.

But the question was discussed before the Royal Commission whether, so far as the Indian government was concerned, free silver was not the best thing. They said it increased the revenue by increasing the exports from India, which pretty nearly balanced the disadvantage. The controversy between them was, whether, so far as the Indian government was concerned, the revenues were so increased by the increase of exports and productions by having cheap money as to make it as easy for them to pay gold interest in cheap silver as it would to pay that gold interest if silver were advanced to par. That was the issue. That was the question discussed. It was left in doubt. But they reviewed the situation, had the evils sufficiently brought before them, and they said that it was a doubtful question whether the

Indian government could carry this additional load better with cheap silver than it could with silver at par.

But there was one question about which there was no doubt, namely: that England was a creditor nation; that all the world were contributing to her wealth; that anything that would increase the amount of money in the world and make it cheaper would be very prejudicial to the bondholders of England, for whom the whole world were laboring; and that was the argument which prevented the conference from recommending the remonetization of silver.

Now, so far as we are concerned, in competition with India we are the sufferers, as was pointed out by the witnesses before the Royal Commission. The average price of a bushel of wheat in London during the last twenty-five years has been 1 ounce of silver. That is shown by the market reports. Now, an ounce of silver in India can be coined into what is equivalent to about $1.37. In the United States an ounce of silver is worth only 88 cents. So when we sell our wheat for an ounce of silver we get 88 cents in our money, and when the Indian farmer sells a bushel of wheat for an ounce of silver he gets $1.37 in his money. And silver, so far as the production of wheat is concerned in India, according to the testimony before the Royal Commission and according to all the testimony we have on the subject, has practically the same purchasing power that it had before the demonetization of silver in the western world.

The exports of wheat from India to Europe have increased from nothing, when silver was at par, to fifty or sixty millions of bushels, and are increasing every year. I think the amount was 50,000,000 bushels this year.

Mr. McPHERSON. Does that make the same condition as to purchasing power as when we had free coinage?

Mr. STEWART. If an ounce of silver was worth, as it would be under free coinage, $1.2929, then you would get $1.2929 instead of 88 cents for wheat in London.

Mr. McPHERSON. Would you get $1.2929 measured in wheat?

Mr. STEWART. Measured in anything. You would get that for your wheat, and when you came back you would have so much more money for production.

So it is with cotton. The building up of the cotton industry and the production of cotton in India is fast supplanting cotton in this country. It is not so good as ours, but for the coarse manufactures it answers the same purpose.

So that it is the policy of England to develop, as they say, agricultural production in other parts of the world so as to keep themselves from paying tribute to the United States. But the United States is just playing into their hands. It is a debtor nation. It has got to buy gold, and sell its products for what it can get, in competition with India.

Mr. PEFFER. Mr. President, I desire to ask the Senator from Nevada whether it is not a fact that the rapid increase in the wheat production of India was not contemporaneous with the demonetization of silver in this country.

Mr. STEWART. It was; it commenced at that time. and it is pointed to by all English financiers as one of the results of that act. Nobody denies that it is one of the results of rejecting silver. It

515

was one of the reasons for demonetizing silver, one of the reasons for not remonetizing it, one of the benefits to counteract the disadvantages of the gold interest that India was bound to pay.

Again, when you come to consider manufacturing the demonetization of silver benefited India, and that was one of the grievances of the English manufacturer. The cotton product of India is increasing so rapidly that she is taking away the English market in China. One hundred million dollars of Indian manufactures of cotton went to China and the East last year, and that was because they could manufacture with cheap money.

The same is true in Mexico. Smelting works and other business establishments are being erected there, because Mexico has plenty of money. I was astonished to see how our American people were viewing the question as regards Mexico. Then, if protection is a good thing, cheap money is a good thing, because what is bought from abroad must be paid for in gold prices, which amounts to a tariff. But India and Mexico buy little from abroad, no more than they are compelled to buy.

India is now manufacturing her own commodities, and that was another cause for complaint at this Manchester meeting of the textile fabric manufacturers. They complained because India could manufacture cheaper than they could; and not only manufacture for themselves, but also for China and the East.

Why, you can do nothing without money. Take money away from a country and you leave it in a helpless condition. That is not the case with the people of India. Those reports that were read by the Senator from Ohio have reference to the disadvantages of the office-holding class with fixed salaries and the Government when required to pay gold interest. Young Englishmen are unwilling to go there to take the place of others on salaries payable in silver. That is the situation.

Mr. SHERMAN told us he knew all about council bills, and I supposed he was going to tell us something about them. I think he forgot it, however, for he did not tell us anything about them. Those bills are used for several purposes. They are sold through the Bank of England, by the order of the Indian council that governs India, upon the English markets, to whoever may buy. They are orders for silver money in India. Any person who wants to transmit money to India to pay for anything buys those bills and sends them there for that purpose. The interest on the Indian debt, the most of which is payable in gold in London, is paid by the sale of these bills. That amounts to about $80,000,000 a year.

Then there are other remittances which have to be made for the purchase of commodities, and which are also paid for in these bills. They have a managing man, a minister of finance, of this Indian government or Indian council, who sells those bills at his discretion, exercising a discretion something like that of the Secretary of the Treasury in selling bonds. When silver goes up he can sell a little more than the market needs, and that is what he does; that is what the English financiers boast of doing as a means of depressing the price of silver. That is the way it embarrasses the market. They have the power to destroy the market. No one dares to compete with the English Government in this business.

The gold trust have prevented India from taking the same amount of silver that she formerly had taken. so as to keep silver down. They published in the papers that they had a way of keeping silver down that Americans did not understand when the act of 1890 was pending. I have not been able to get at the data exactly, but I know that they issue paper in India, uncovered paper money, a certain amount of rupees, and they can put out a little of that and ease matters. There are various ways of keeping silver down and they have .nanaged this whole business.

There is not in all this world more than $10,000,000, and I do not believe there is in the world more than $6,000,000, of silver bullion. The Senator from Ohio proposes to bring down the price of $4,000,000,000 of legal-tender silver which is circulating in the world and doing money duty as legal-tender money to the level of this speculative bullion that is kept in the markets as a sinker. His object is to keep down the price of an ounce of silver so that Europe may continue to get cheap silver from the United States. That is what he wants, and that is the way those who have this matter in charge manage it. If this little surplus were taken out of the market silver would be at par.

If there had been no manipulation to prevent exports of silver to India, silver would have been at par under the act of 1890. The exports to India were decreased by English management as much as our purchases were increased by that act.

Since 1850, as I stated yesterday, the ratio of production has been 40 of silver to 60 of gold. There has been no surplus of silver produced in the world. All of it was consumed until the agitation in 1890 put it up, making it necessary for Great Britain to take this action. During nine months of the last fiscal year the exports of India fell off $17,000,000, which, if continued at the same rate during the whole year, would make about $24,000,-000 or $25,000,000. This reduction in the consumption of India would about equal our increased purchases.

Now, we are told that the silver money of the world shall be brought down to its market value. What does that mean? It means a contraction of the world's money at once of at least $1,-300,000,000. The recoinage of the silver coin of the world at this other ratio would entail a loss of fully 33⅓ per cent, and in the four thousand millions that loss would amount to something over $1,300,000,000. Who would lose the $1,300,000,000? The people who have the silver coin, because silver is the people's money. Who would make it? The gold trust, because gold is the money of the rich. Must we pay this bonus to be liberated from the crime of 1873? Is not that robbery? Have the gold kings got us in a position where they can say ''Stand and deliver?''

The Senator from Ohio tells us that silver is too heavy to use, and yet he proposes to add 33⅓ per cent to the weight of the dollar! Anything, no matter in what shape it comes, which will liberate the people from the tyranny of the gold trust has in all forms and under all circumstances met with his determined opposition. He made one mistake, but he did not know it: I do not think he took advice on it. He consented to the law of 1890, which makes further legislation necessary. We have $500,000,000 of silver now and we have nothing with which to redeem it; we have no gold with which to redeem it. We can not keep it up in that way. There is no law to purchase gold, and it becomes necessary for us to sustain silver, and the load is increasing year by year.

I voted for the act of 1890 because I believed it would create the necessity for legislation for free coinage, and that the whole world would see it. When we get three or four hundred millions more of silver and have no gold in the Treasury, I think we shall have some interest in putting up the price of silver and in using it as money and paying it out. I think we shall have to do that. I think we can hardly remain in partnership with Great Britain in the effort to put down and disparage silver. I think it was a great wrong for a debtor nation to enter into these schemes to increase our obligations and rob the people, and I think that the partnership between the Treasury Department and the Bank of England will have to be dissolved by the operation of the act of 1890. I like to see the load piling up, and hear the agents of the gold trust talking about carrying it with gold. The load will soon be too heavy. The gold wheels are not strong enough. The old silver wheels must be put back or there will be a financial breakdown.

That was my view of that bill when it passed, and it is still my view, and I glory in it. It was all we could get, but we got something that makes them talk nonsense, makes them talk about buying gold to sustain silver, when they have no authority to do it. The Secretary of the Treasury is in great distress, and we are told he has a busy day in Wall street, consulting how to maintain the credit of this Government. How humiliating! If this were not a great and serious question it would be comical to see the Secretary dodging around those banking establishments, asking them to keep the United States Government from bankruptcy and at the same time secure to the money-loaners two dollars for one and make the people submit to it. That would be really comical if it did not grind the life and energy out of the American people, and if it did not take hundreds of millions of discount each year to keep up this tyranny.

Then we are told that we propose to rob the soldier, the pensioner. How pathetic was the Senator from Ohio! How mournful was the extract he read from Mr. Harter! The poor soldier! The poor soldier is going to be robbed unless the people are denied money altogether. Unless the value of gold is doubled up each year for the benefit of the gold trusts, the poor soldier will be robbed! I think we can take care of the soldier with silver money. I think he will take that if he can buy with it what he wants to eat and drink, etc. I do not think the soldier wants to see the farmer, his neighbor, driven into bankruptcy, his children go uneducated, and general misery and gloom rest upon the country merely for the purpose of drawing a gold dollar, when a silver dollar is just as good.

The soldier fought for his country. He liberated 4,000,000 blacks. Has he become so unpatriotic as to desire that 65,000,000 of American citizens, including whites and blacks, shall be reduced to slavery by the kings of avarice?

His sacrifices were great and his achievements glorious for liberty. He never will be the instrument of extortion from the American people. He was too brave a man, and he likes to see prosperity in the community; he likes to see his neighbor get

good prices for his wheat and cotton, and he is generally patriotic and honest.

But how has this gold trust treated the soldier heretofore?
Has it ever been tenderhearted to him? It paid him in greenbacks during the war, and his wife and family had only greenbacks to use. while it paid gold to the money-lender, which is
worth now three or four times as much as the greenbacks were
when the soldiers were paid.

Is not this a shame? Is it not an outrage after having paid the
soldier in depreciated greenbacks, and after having changed the
contracts in the bonds which were also payable in greenbacks,
to gold contracts and defrauded the people, that these gold sharks
should try to deceive the soldiers?

The soldiers have lost heavily by the policy which has been
pursued. They are enterprising people; they have lost by the
depreciation of property, by the stagnation of business, $10 where
they will make one in pensions by this scheme. A more pre-
posterous humbug never was invented. The soldier does not
want to deprive the people of money. What he gets in the way
of pension does not support him and he has to make something
outside of that. He does not want stagnation and hard times, he
is not a money shark, he is not a money dealer; he is satisfied
with a good silver dollar. Give him back the silver dollar of
the fathers, which has been current from the foundation of the
Government, and he will be satisfied. He is not complaining.
Mr. HARTER invented this piece of sentimentalism, and the Senator from Ohio, who likes sentimentalism, adopted it.

Then, again, the Senator refers to the savings deposits of the
laboring classes, and says they are going to be ruined. With a
million of men out of employment, how much are they ruined every
day? It is said they have $3,000,000,000 in savings banks. There
are more than a million of men out of employment. Two million
or three million men more would be employed if business was
lively. They would have something then to deposit.

Are the laboring classes benefited by contraction and hard
times and starvation in the country? They are the people upon
whom the iron hand of contraction first falls and reduces their
wages. It is true our labor organizations in this country have
braced up a little. They can not be treated as they are in Europe;
they can not be shot down on the street, but the iron hand of
contraction crushes everything. When you have destroyed
enough business enterprises to have no labor, these men have
got to starve or work for such wages as they can get, as in other
countries.

Talk about contraction for the benefit of labor! Talk about
the corner in gold for the benefit of laborers! The man who so
speaks, speaks in the interest of extortion. He does not care a
baubee for the laborer; he has no human heart to sympathize
with mankind. A man who is patriotic and good wants all the
world to prosper, he wants fair play and honest dealing. The
soldiers and the laborers called in as allies to oppress the people
in favor of the money dealer! It is desired to have more of this
tentative legislation under which the few have become rich and
the many are impoverished.

What ought to be the condition of mankind to-day, with universal peace, with abundant harvests for twenty-five years, and with an abundant supply of the precious metals? If the traditions of the fathers had been adhered to the progress of the world during these twenty-five years would have been unparalleled. What occurred in the first twenty-five years after the discovery of gold? I wish I could command the language to describe that eventful period as it has been described by some. In the beginning of that period Sir Archibald Alison told what it would be. He foretold the horrors of contraction from 1810 to 1850. He told of the attempts which were made to invent devices of all kinds to prevent the difficulty. Some proposed free trade and some protection. The world tried these experiments for half a century. The hand of Providence was stretched out and granted the relief which made prosperity universal. The new discoveries of precious metals breathed life into the channels of trade. They transformed society from a state of despondency to a condition of hope and prosperity.

I have not language adequate to describe what occurred in those twenty-five years. The progress in civilization, and the advance in the arts, invention, and the improvement of mankind, have no parallel in history; no century can compare with it. But since this crime of 1873 was perpetrated, we have been struggling against a contracting currency until we have got pretty near the end of the tether, and the word has gone forth that credit everywhere must be curtailed, that enterprise must cease. To save whom? To save the money-loaners, to save their reserves. How they talk about their reserves and how they collect the last dollar! They have even threatened for the last three or four years to make poor Austria come into this scheme and buy gold. She tried it a little this spring. It commenced pinching elsewhere for money in the money markets, and they became alarmed and gave her a little more time. It was said she should buy in the first place $200,000,000 of gold, which would be 6 per cent of all the gold in the world. She took five or six millions from here. The money kings said "We must not go too fast; we will bankrupt our debtors and lose our money. We must make this squeeze gradual."

We must prevent discussion on this subject, the Senator from Ohio tells us; we must only let the wise men discuss it, and not let the people look into it; a few wise men can devise a scheme to bridge things a'ong, contract the currency, bleed the people, and reduce them by degrees to submission. If this condition had been produced in a day there would have been war in this country. It took years to reduce the people to a condition of dependence.

The Senator from Ohio referred to homesteads. I should like to discuss the homestead question. I had almost forgotten that. Nine-tenths of them are mortgaged and in the hands of the money sharks all over the country, and under this form of contraction they will eventually take the rest. That is the love they have for the homesteaders; that is the sentimental regard which the Senator from Ohio has for the homesteaders. He was afraid the values of homesteads would fall so low that the mortgagees would not get their money. The idea of money sharks having friendship for homestead settlers when they have taken away from them their property, which is going into the hands of the few constantly!

Take up any State of the Union and the homesteads will not bring to-day under the hammer 50 cents on the dollar of what they would eighteen years ago. Take any of the homesteads in Virginia, and you will find that they are greatly reduced in value. That is what these sharks are aiming at, to reduce the value of the farms; that is what they are after. The idea of a gold contractionist having sympathy with the homesteaders! Sympathy! There is not blood enough in all of them for one mosquito. [Laughter.]

The Senator says that if we should have free coinage of silver it would stop the coinage of gold. Then, what will they do with gold? What use will they have for it? It would be just where silver is now. That is just what Chevalier and the cunning ones of Europe attempted to do with gold, to demonetize it. They were frank about it. Ninety-nine one-hundreths of the demand for gold is a money demand. Take away the money demand for gold and there is one hundred years' supply of that metal on hand for other purposes than money. What will you do with it? Gold with that supply on hand would not be worth more than $2 a pound. We could not coin it the Senator from Ohio says. He says we would be fools to coin it. I think they would be fools not to coin it. I do not think they are as big fools as that. They used to coin it when they coined silver. There was no trouble about it then.

The logic of the Senator's speech is amusing to me. The people want more money and not cheaper money, the Senator says. I should like to know how they can accomplish that. When they are able to do that they can raise themselves by their bootstraps or fly up in the air. "More money and not cheaper money!" The Senator speaks as if money was not governed by the same law of supply and demand that governs everything else. If there is more money in the market certainly it will be cheaper. Money is worth twice as much as it was eighteen years ago, while property is not worth more than half as much. Why is that? It is because there is less money; it has gone up. Silver has not gone down, as compared with property, but the price of gold has gone up. There has been a great demand for gold, and its value has doubled in the last eighteen years.

Then the Senator says we can have more money and have it just as dear. He wants to hold on to the grasp he has on his victim: he does not want to let his victim loose one instant.

The Senator talks about the purchasing power of money. That will not do. The logic of more money and not decreasing its purchasing power is new. Now, he says that the Government of the United States has got great credit, and they can fix up some credit scheme that will make it all right: just wait and let it be done by wise men, knowing men, and we will fix up a credit scheme, and make it payable in gold. We will not have any more gold than we have now, but we will fix it so that we will get along nicely if we will trust wise financiers!

What act of finance for the last thirty years has been passed that has any philosophy in it? Take the banking act. It was a makeshift; it was enacted for the purpose of allowing the bankers to speculate, and get a subsidy. At first they got $15,-

000,000 a year. They bought their bonds, deposited them in the Treasury, drew 90 per cent of currency, then circulated that, and they could take that 90 per cent and buy more bonds, and they went right on buying bonds. It was a wonderfully rich thing for them, but it had no element of perpetuity in it. It was one of these tentative schemes, because it was only devised to last while the debt remained unpaid; it was not intended as a permanent money scheme at all. It left the expansion and contraction in the hands of a ring, and gave the ring a subsidy. That is what it did.

Then the next tentative scheme, after they had got the people largely in debt and received large claims against them, was to destroy one-half the world's money. So they have gone on with their tentative schemes of robbery and their experiments to see how much the people would endure. The Senator from Ohio says these ephemeral schemes are very wise because they are experimental; you are not committed to them; you merely try them until you exhaust the patience of the people!

I am opposed to trying any more new experiments. I want to return to the gold and silver which was the foundation of credit and which was money from prehistoric times. I am opposed to these experiments. They have been so illogical, they have been so destructive of human happiness, so detrimental to progress, that I am tired of them.

The Senator says this is a Presidential year, and if we discuss the situation in the Senate it may prevent somebody getting elected to the Presidency. Had not the people better understand this question before they vote? Had they not better know that we are on the eve of bankruptcy and that something must be done? Had they not better know that the financial condition of the world is tending to inevitable ruin in the attempt to buy gold when we can not get it? Had they not better know what this question is and take such action as will avoid the threatened calamity?

The United States can maintain free coinage alone, There is no doubt of it. There is only $10,000,000 of bullion to take care of. The idea that silver will come here is nonsense. As I said yesterday, why did not France sell the $120,000,000 of silver which she holds of the other members of the Latin Union which, according to agreement. they were required to redeem in gold at $1.33 an ounce. if she was so anxious to get rid of it?

Then they tell us that Roumania has threatened to sell $25,000,000 of silver and some other countries $5,000,000. Suppose they succeeded in their threat, it would not be a drop in the bucket. All the silver in Europe which is referred to in the speech of the Senator is only about $75,000.000. That is not as much as the gold we disposed of in six months.

A flood of silver! It must be taken from the mountains and by slow processes. When they tell you it is easily produced, they tell you what is false. Silver is hard to produce. As one mine is found another is exhausted, and it requires continual work to keep the mines going. It is no exaggeration to say that every ounce of silver costs $4 to produce. There can not be much in it. There is no danger of a flood. The precious metals are hard to get. The increase since 1852 has been only forty or fifty million dollars, taking the two metals at their coinage value. There has been a very slow increase; it is hard to produce; and that is the reason why the quantity is necessarily limited.

I say that the product we have had of the precious metals should have given us good times. We must come back to free coinage. There is not too much silver produced. The United States needs about $500,000,000 of the precious metals to put behind our paper to secure a metallic basis dollar for dollar. Suppose we should put silver behind the paper, we could not get enough to be dollar for dollar in twenty years and supply other countries. There is no trouble about it at all. Everybody knows that there will be a scanty supply for the United States even with free coinage.

But it is said we must consult Europe, that we must take orders from Europe, that we can not have an independent financial policy of our own; that we must depend upon the bankers of Europe to legislate for us, and that we must have an international monetary conference. I should like to see a commission if it were honestly constituted. But suppose two men are appointed on that commission, if it is composed of only three, or three men, if it is to be composed of five, who know nothing about the question, who are bankers, who are in the interest of the gold ring, who know nothing about the question, but will do what they are told, what good would be accomplished? There is hardly a banker in the United States who has ever properly investigated this question. Bankers want to get all they can and they do what they are told. Their attention is usually directed to the discovery of the best process for squeezing the people. They have no sentiment for mankind.

If there is good faith in the proposed international conference no man should be appointed as a member of it who is not heartily in favor of the free coinage of silver in America, who does not believe in silver equally with gold, and who has not studied the subject so as to understand all its details, to answer any question which may be propounded, and expose the sophistries of the monometallists. We want no Turveydrops who follow the platitudes of the gold ring. It is no evidence that men are good because they claim to be good, that they are honest because they claim to be honest. It would be difficult to find a rascal who did not do most of his evil deeds in the name of virtue. He would be a novelty. The very fact that the worst gold conspirator in America will claim that he is a bimetallist proves that bimetallism is right and its opponents are wrong. They stand before the country condemned by their own confession. You can not know them by their words; it is by their acts you shall know them.

I did not intend to detain the Senate so long, and should not have done so but for the reason that this subject is so far-reaching, it is so important, it is so essential to the prosperity of the country. It is wicked to oppress the people when we have all the means of prosperity at hand. It is wicked that a generation which has been born to an inheritance of the precious metals denied to all others, should be subjected to all the pains and penalties of money contraction. How long the people will submit to it I do not know, but while I live I shall continue to warn them of this

monster evil. It may be too great to resist. I have been often
told that it was, and that I was throwing away my time in telling the truth, but I do not believe it.

I believe that we shall have free coinage of silver, and I believe we shall have it in the near future. I believe that the
people are getting sufficient intelligence to demand it. I believe
the demand for it will come with emphasis, and that very soon.
These questions go on in this way until they culminate; and
when the people of this country are once aroused they are able
to meet every emergency.

My people smart under the abuse they receive from Senators
in this Chamber and from the public press. See their condition.
They were the pioneers who developed the far West; they were
the pioneers who poured the treasure of the new world of the
West into the lap of the old world of the East; they were the
pioneers who made it possible for us to have a financial system
which could sustain this Government during the war.

How well I remember when I first came to Washington in the
winter of 1864-'65 and called on Mr. Lincoln. He took me by
both hands. and said he, "I am glad to see you. You come
from a country which has given us the means to preserve this
Union. If it had not been for the gold and silver we got from
California, Nevada, and the other Pacific States and Territories
we could not have maintained our credit, and all would have
been lost." Said he: "I feel grateful to the pioneers of that
country who have done so much in the development of the gold
and silver mines." He said further: "I am told your Comstock
is going to be a great mine; that others are being discovered,
and the prospect of being relieved of our financial difficulties is
brightened by it."

At that time, when we had laid the foundation of an empire in
that country, when we had invested our labor and spent our lives
in laying the financial basis for this country, we were receiving
the friendship and the plaudits of all the world. We are now
denounced as dishonest because we protest against the crime of
1873. Is it not enough to arouse the spirit of any American who
loves justice and hates fraud and tyranny, after our property has
been taken from us, and after we saved the country from ruin by
our enterprise, to be called dishonest and to be sneered at in this
Chamber as advocating local interests, when we are advocating
the interest of mankind?

I repel these insults in the name of my people, in the name of
justice, and shall continue to repel them. The monopolists and
contractionists will find that the men in the mountains will yet
be heard from. They have been robbed, their fortunes have
been taken from them, their property has been confiscated, and
for whom? For the money-loaner. But what our people have
lost has been a mere bagatelle to the vast millions which the
producers of the South and West have lost by being compelled
to discount their property to buy gold to enrich the gold trust
who have a monopoly of the gold of the world. Ah, it will not
do for these robbers—for they are nothing else as the result
shows—to claim for themselves all the honesty. Honesty is ban-
ished from the world when the crime of 1873 is justified! ·

www.ingramcontent.com/pod-product-compliance
Lightning Source LLC
Chambersburg PA
CBHW032134080426
42733CB00008B/1068